THIRTEEN LESSONS
ON
GALATIANS

Bible Student Study Guide

THIRTEEN LESSONS ON GALATIANS

by

Kenny Boles

College Press, Joplin, Missouri

Copyright © 1978
College Press Publishing Company

Second Printing - 1980
Third Printing - 1988

Printed and Bound in the
United States of America

All Rights Reserved

International Standard Book Number: 0-89900-158-0

Contents

Introduction	v
Preface	vi
LESSON 1 — Galatians 1:1-10	1
LESSON 2 — Galatians 1:11-24	8
LESSON 3 — Galatians 2:1-10	14
LESSON 4 — Galatians 2:11-21	20
LESSON 5 — Galatians 3:1-14	27
LESSON 6 — Galatians 3:15-29	33
LESSON 7 — Galatians 4:1-16	41
LESSON 8 — Galatians 4:17-31	47
LESSON 9 — Galatians 5:1-15	54
LESSON 10 — Galatians 5:16-21	60
LESSON 11 — Galatians 5:22-26	67
LESSON 12 — Galatians 6:1-10	73
LESSON 13 — Galatians 6:11-18	79

Introduction

The Christians of Galatia were deserting the faith! They had come to know God's grace through Paul's own preaching, and now they were turning away. No longer trusting in the death of Jesus to win their salvation, they were turning back to works of law. No longer believing that Jesus paid it all, they were frantically trying to furnish part of the price themselves. Christ had set them free, but they were choosing to go back under the yoke of slavery. Paul's task was clear: Rescue the Galatians from the chains of legalism, and restore them in the grace of Christ.

The book of Galatians seems to divide naturally into three parts:

> Apostleship — chapters 1 & 2
> Arguments — chapters 3 & 4
> Application — chapters 5 & 6

First, Paul proves his right to be called an apostle, in order to defend the truth of his gospel. Second, Paul presents a number of arguments to prove that the law of the old covenant has given way to the grace of the new. Third, Paul shows how this freedom in Christ is to be applied in our own lives.

For convenience in study, this workbook has been divided into thirteen lessons. Each lesson will have the scripture text, explanations of each

THIRTEEN LESSONS ON GALATIANS

verse, and questions to stimulate your thinking.

Finally, remember that legalism is not easily stamped out. Long after Paul wrote Galatians, Martin Luther still had to do battle with the "work your way into forgiveness" system. We are also confronted with the same battle today. It is of crucial importance that every one of us should face the question of law versus grace, and come to the right conclusions. Perhaps this workbook can help you do this very thing. May God bless your study.

Preface

LAW OR GRACE

by

Seth Wilson

The law was given through Moses; grace and truth came through Jesus Christ (John 1:17).

The New Testament plainly teaches what every Christian needs to know: that the religion which is by faith in Jesus Christ is separate and distinct from the Old Testament. It is not only a new covenant in place of the old one, but it is also one of a different kind. Even the Old Testament plainly declared that it would be so. Read Jeremiah 31:31-34 and the comments on it in Hebrews 8:1-13.

Christ Fulfilled the Law

Jesus came not to destroy the law but to fulfill it (Matt. 5:17), and He did fulfill it!

He fulfilled it as a promise or note is fulfilled when it is paid in full. He brought, or did, or was, what the Old Testament promised and predicted.

He fulfilled it as a set of blueprints is fulfilled when the house is completed. He established what the Old Testament outlined and fore-patterned in type and shadow.

He fulfilled it as the apple fulfills the apple blossom. The Old Testament was as necessary in preparing for Christ and the gospel as the blossom is in preparing for the apple. But, as the appleblossom disappears when the apple develops, not being destroyed or made void, but being fulfilled and validated by the apple which displaces it, so also the law is not destroyed, but is made valid by the Christ who furnishes, and is, what it prepared for.

He manifested in His life the righteousness the law described.

He bore in His death the punishment the law inflicted. He fulfilled the sentence it pronounced against sinners. Thus He upheld the validity of its demands and established its divine authority; but at the same time, He satisfied its claims and dismissed its charge against us. He nailed it to the cross (Col. 2:14).

A New Covenant

After the death of Jesus, a new will (or testament) was proclaimed from heaven; and by it the former will is made obsolete and no longer binding.

In the book of Acts we see the new covenant in effect. We also see some men trying to perpetuate the old covenant even in the church. They tried to mingle together the rule of Christ and the rule of the law. But God revealed that they do not mix.

First, the benefits of the gospel were proclaimed to all in Judea without regard to how well they had kept the law. Then God expressly directed that it was to be preached to Gentiles without the law (Acts 10:1 to 11:18). Still later when some tried to lay upon the Gentile Christians an obligation to the law, the will of the Lord was revealed that it was not to be so (Acts 15:1-31).

Still, often and in many places the problem arose, for the advocates of the law were not easily convinced, and human nature is inclined to legalism. So the truth and grace of Christ versus the bondage and failure of the law, as a way of life and righteousness, was often discussed in Paul's epistles: especially in Romans, Galatians, Colossians, and Hebrews, but also in others.

Note some of the many ways in which the Spirit of God says that the law came to an end and was displaced by the gospel of Christ: "Ye are not under the law" (Gal. 5:18; 3:23-25). "Ye are not under law, but under grace" (Rom. 6:14). "Ye also were made dead to the law . . . that ye should be joined to another" (Rom. 7:4). "I died unto the law, that I might live unto God" (Gal. 2:19-21). "We have been discharged from the law, having died to that wherein ye were held" (Rom. 7:6). "It is done away in Christ" (II Cor. 3:14). He "abolished . . . the law" (Eph. 2:14-15). He "blotted out" the law, "and he hath taken it out of the way, nailing it to the cross" (Col. 2:14). He "made of necessity a change . . . of the law" (Heb. 7:12). "There is a disannulling of a foregoing commandment because of its weakness and unprofitableness" (Heb. 7:18). "He taketh away the first (covenant) that he may establish the second" (Heb. 10:9).

There can be no doubt that some law was abrogated; but there is often disagreement as to what it was. In II Cor. 3:1-14 the old covenant which was done away is expressly stated to be that which was written on tables of stone when Moses' face was shining (that is, the Ten Commandments). According to the letter of the apostles and elders in Acts 15:22-29, the Gentile Christians were not expected to observe anything of the Jewish law or customs except to abstain from blood, idols, from things strangled, and fornication. In Galatians 2:3; 5:2-6; I Cor. 7:18-19 circumcision is especially mentioned as a key element of that which was no more binding upon men; and circumcision was given to Abraham long before Moses' time. Paul says that if anyone accepts circumcision, as a religious obligation, he becomes obligated to do the whole law (Gal. 5:3); thus he makes it all a unit. Although we may regard part of the law as ceremonial and other parts as moral law, such a distinction is never made or even assumed in Scripture.

Several passages, such as Rom. 6:14-15; 10:4; Gal. 2:16, 19, 21; 5:18, 23, use no article "the" with the word "law" in the original language; thus they say that we are not under law anymore, speaking of law in general as a principle or method by which God deals with men. They probably refer to the Mosaic law as the outstanding example of law, but they speak broadly of the nature of any legal system.

The Christian is simply not under anything but Christ (read Col. 2:8 to 3:17). "Christ is the end of law (no article) for righteousness to every one that believeth" (Rom. 10:4).

A New Kind of Covenant

The gospel of Christ is not simply another law or a better law, it is something different from law. The gospel did not introduce a new system of right and wrong, but a new way of dealing with it. The rule of Christ is not a reign of law, but the manifestation of a new creature, the product of a new spirit, the working of Christ in us through faith and love (Gal. 5:6, 13-18, 22-25; 6:15-16; Rom. 14:17).

The written record of the law is still valuable. It is useful to reveal sin in its deadly sinfulness, and to show man's need for salvation under some system other than law. It helps to bring us to Christ (Gal. 3:24; II Tim. 3:15). It bears a powerful testimony to the divine origin of the gospel which it predicts and prefigures in so many ways.

But the law, as a covenant under which we have our standing before

God, cannot continue in force over those who are in Christ. If Christians were to try to be justified by the law, they would be fallen away from grace, and Christ would become of none effect to them (Gal. 5:1-6). In the very process of coming into Christ men are made dead to the law. By grace men are brought into a new and different relationship with God, a new condition of heart, and a new kind of control in Christ.

A New Relationship With God

Under law man stands in a legal relationship with God; the law stands between man and God. One's acceptance or condemnation before God is determined rigidly by how he has kept the law. He stands as one who merits all he receives, boasting before God (a sad distortion of goodness!). Or rather, acutally, through lack of merit, he is unable to stand at all. Cursed is everyone who does not do *all* the law *all* the time (Gal. 3:10; James 2:10). By works of law no man can be justified before God (Rom. 3:19-20; Gal. 2:16; 3:11; Acts 13:39). Under law anyone who feels justified can do so only by blinding himself to the meaning of the law and the condition of his own heart and life. The law can be nothing else than a "ministration of death" and "condemnation" (II Cor. 3:7, 9); for it can only declare the guilt and pronounce the doom of sinners. It cannot make alive. The law makes a just and righteous demand upon men; but it does not enable them to do and be what is demanded.

Under grace, our relationship with God is quite different, not on the basis of how we have kept the law, but on the fact that we have become united with Christ and are living in Him. It is an entirely personal relationship, by which we accept His offer of loving favor by personal trust in Jesus and by accepting His death, His life, and His leadership for our redemption from sin, our way of life, and our reason to be. By His death on our behalf He fulfilled the sentence of the law against us. We acknowledge the guilt of our sin, accept His death as our death, count ourselves as crucified with Christ, and henceforth live no longer unto ourselves, but unto Him, in Him, and for Him. He is our righteousness before the judgment of God, and He is our way of life here upon the earth. In Him we stand; without Him we perish! The best lawkeeper in the world is just as lost as the worst sinner in hell; but any man who will can have eternal life and the fruits of righteousness in Christ. Under law no one is worthy even to continue in this earthly life. But through yielding in faith and love unto Christ, we are being prepared to share with Him His own infinite and eternal inheritance. This is the power and the glory of God's grace!

Lesson One

(1:1-10)

Salutation (1:1-5)
1 Paul an apostle — not from men nor through man, but through Jesus Christ and God the Father, who raised him from the dead — 2 and all the brethren who are with me,
To the churches of Galatia:
3 Grace to you and peace from God the Father and our Lord Jesus Christ, 4 who gave himself for our sins to deliver us from the present evil age, according to the will of our God and Father; 5 to whom be the glory for ever and ever. Amen.

As Paul reminds us later in this epistle (4:13-19), the Christians in Galatia were his own spiritual children in the faith. Paul is writing, then, to people he loves very deeply. Significantly, however, Paul omits the words of thanksgiving and commendation which usually opens his letters. Because of the gravity of the problem in Galatia, Paul gets right to work.

V. 1 **Paul an apostle** — Until the First Missionary Journey (Acts 13:9) Paul was known by the Hebrew name Saul. It was by this name that we first met him (Acts 7:58) as one who helped in the stoning of Stephen.

1

CHAPTER 1

GALATIANS 1:1-5

The name Paul is a Roman name.

The word "apostle" comes from the Greek word *apostolos* which means "one sent forth." In its special use here in the New Testament it refers to the men personally chosen and sent out by Jesus. Jesus promised these men inspiration (John 14:26) and gave them unique authority in the founding of the church (John 20:21-23; Ephesians 2:20). Paul was chosen to be an apostle by Jesus on the road to Damascus (Acts 26:12-18). Paul will spend most of the next two chapters proving his apostleship.

not from men nor through man — Paul was not like the false apostles (II Cor. 11:13) whose authority was only from men. Neither was he like Matthias (Acts 1:26) who was chosen by God through the agency of men. Paul's calling was directly from God through the Lord Jesus Christ.

raised him from the dead — The Galatians needed more than anything else to learn the significance of Jesus' death, burial, and resurrection. The gospel facts, properly understood, would end forever their turning back to legalism.

V. 2 **and all the brethren** — Paul did not stand alone in the doctrine of salvation by grace instead of works of law. This was the belief of all the church — it was the teaching of the Lord. It was not Paul who was out of step with the Galatians; the Galatians were out of step with all the rest.

the churches of Galatia — It is unlikely that these churches were in that area of central Asia Minor usually marked as Galatia on Bible maps. We have no knowledge of any journeys by Paul into that area. Probably this refers to the area to the south which includes the cities of Derbe, Lystra, Iconium, and Antioch of Pisidia (Acts 13:14—14:23). While some maps mark this as Lycaonia, the political boundaries drawn up by Rome included this area with the area to the north, and called all of it Galatia. It is interesting that Paul was first worshipped, then stoned, at one of these cities (Acts 14:11-19).

V. 3 **Grace to you** — Every one of the thirteen epistles signed by Paul begins and ends with a note of grace. Could it be that a man who had so violently persecuted the church simply felt a greater appreciation for God's grace? The word "grace" is often defined as "unmerited favor." What this means is that although we are unworthy and undeserving, God likes us anyway! Grace is goodwill, favor, and lovingkindness — to people who do not deserve it.

and peace — Peace is best defined as "well-being of the soul." The Christian has inner peace because there is first peace with God through the sacrifice of Christ. This is of utmost importance in the Galatian problem of legalism.

It has often been noted that "grace" (*charis*) is very similar in Greek to the usual Greek greeting (*chairein*). Also, "peace" was the usual

CHAPTER 1   GALATIANS 1:1-5

Hebrew greeting (*shalom*). Since so much of Paul's ministry involved bringing together Jews and Greeks into one body (Eph. 3:6-7), it seems somehow appropriate that this Greek-Jew greeting should begin each of his epistles.

God the Father — Paul speaks of the Father three times in these opening verses. Perhaps this helps prepare the way for the arguments for our sonship through Christ in chapters three and four.

our Lord Jesus Christ — The title "Lord" is used in Greek for an owner of property; a master of slaves; a deity to be worshipped. It was even used in the Greek translation of the Old Testament in place of the unspeakable name Jehovah or Yahweh. The Lord Jesus is the Lord of all lords (Rev. 19:16). Consider all that the title "Lord" implies, then read Luke 6:46.

"Jesus" was the historical name given by the angel to both Mary (Luke 1:31) and Joseph (Matt. 1:21). It is the same as the Old Testament name Joshua, and means "Jehovah is salvation."

"Christ" simply means "anointed," and is the equivalent of the Hebrew word "Messiah." In the Old Testament, reference is made to the anointing of prophets (Isa. 61:1), priests (Exod. 29:7), and kings (I Sam. 15:1). The long-awaited Messiah or Christ was anointed our great Prophet, Priest, and King.

V. 4 **who gave himself for our sins** — Jesus carried our sins to the cross to pay the penalty for our sins (I Pet. 2:24 and Rom. 6:23). The question which must be answered by the Galatians and all other legalists is this: Did Jesus succeed in the mission to the cross, or not? If Jesus paid for our sins, we cannot. If Jesus failed to pay for our sins, we must try to do it ourselves. And we will do this with the sentence of death hanging over us at the first wrong step (Gal. 3:10).

to deliver us — The Greek word for "deliver" meant literally "to snatch out." The book of Acts provides an excellent commentary on this word, using it in these ways:
        a. The rescue of Joseph from his afflictions (7:10).
        b. The deliverance of Israel from Egypt (7:34).
        c. The rescue of Peter from prison (12:11).
        d. The rescue of Paul from the temple mob (23:27).
        e. The deliverance of Paul from the Jews (26:17).

from the present evil age — Long before Jesus came the Jews spoke of two ages. The first was characterized by evil and was the age in which they lived. The second would be known for righteousness and would be ushered in by the Messiah. Paul is pointing out, then, that the Messiah has come and the rescue has been accomplished.

according to the will of our God and Father — It is not God's will that any man should perish, but rather that every man should come to repentance and be saved (II Pet. 3:9).

V. 5 **to whom be the glory** — The word "glory" is surrounded with the imagery of light. It pictures God as clothed in radiance, splendor, and magnificance. Glory must be recognized as rightly belonging only to God. Honor and praise did not belong to Paul (1:10, 24) or the church leaders in Jerusalem (2:6) or to the false teachers (4:17). The glory belongs to God through Christ (6:14)!

No Other Gospel (1:6-10)

6 I am astonished that you are so quickly deserting him who called you in the grace of Christ and turning to a different gospel — 7 not that there is another gospel, but there are some who trouble you and want to pervert the gospel of Christ. 8 But even if we, or an angel from heaven, should preach to you a gospel contrary to that which we preached to you, let him be accursed. 9 As we have said before, so now I say again, If any one is preaching to you a gospel contrary to that which you received, let him be accursed.

10 Am I now seeking the favor of men, or of God? Or am I trying to please men? If I were still pleasing men, I should not be a servant of Christ.

V. 6 **I am astonished** — Paul has just finished the shortest and least complimentary of all his introductory greetings. Now, the very first word is: "I am astonished!" How very much like a parent who is scolding a child for his shockingly wrong behavior! Perhaps a very gradual, slow decline into false doctrine is understandable, but this had happened in a very few years.

so quickly deserting — The word "deserting" involves a fundamental change in character, as when Jezebel "changed" Ahab (I Kg. 21:25). In secular Greek history, when Dionysius deserted the Stoics and went over to the Epicureans (notice Acts 17:18), he was called "the Turncoat" or "Traitor." The word used for his reversal of attitude is here applied to the Galatians.

him who called you in the grace of Christ — This probably refers to the Father (1:15-16), although it could also refer to Paul himself. The important point is this: In turning away from the one who called them, they were abandoning the grace of Christ.

turning to a different gospel — The King James Version is confusing at this point. (". . . unto another gospel: which is not another.") Two separate Greek words are used, making an important distinction. In verse six it is a "different" (*heteros*) gospel to which they turned. In verse seven they are told that their gospel is not "another-of-the-same-kind" (*allos*) gospel.

CHAPTER 1   GALATIANS 1:6-10

V. 7 **not that there is another gospel** — There is only one gospel, and it is the gospel of grace. How long will people go on in their dangerous folly, "It doesn't matter what you believe."? Worse yet was the false view of certain Galatians that the gospel of law-keeping was the only truth.

some who trouble you — Paul refers several times to the false teachers operating in Galatia, but he never pinpoints them by name. He chose rather to describe their doctrine and to warn Christians to beware of any teachers who match the description.

want to pervert the gospel of Christ — By adding the rite of circumcision and other works of law to the gospel, the false teachers were making much more than a minor alteration. As the Greek word implies, they were "completely turning around" the gospel truth. Their "good news" was bad news.

V. 8 **even if we, or an angel from heaven** — The faith has been "once for all delivered to the saints" (Jude 3). No one — not even apostles or angels — can change it. Even if an angel actually did appear to Joseph Smith, founder of the Mormons, it still would not matter. The gospel cannot be changed. We can neither add to it teachings of our own liking, nor can we subtract from it whatever does not please us.

a gospel contrary to that which we preached — Please remember the context of this well-known passage. The gospel contrary to the truth was the gospel of legalism. How awful that some of the worst legalists in the world should seize this verse to serve themselves! Preaching the very gospel Paul condemned, they then boldly proclaim, "And if anyone preaches anything contrary to what we preach, let him be accursed!"

let him be accursed — To be "accursed" meant to be "set up" to God. The same word was used in reference to the city of Jericho before its destruction by Joshua (Joshua 6:18). The city and all its contents were to be destroyed, according to the will of God. We should view all those who pervert the gospel as people marked by God for ultimate destruction.

V. 9 **so now I say again** — The solemn repetition of the warning accentuates the gravity of the matter. Let no man miss the point!

If any one is preaching to you — There is a subtle, but important, difference between the warnings of verse 8 and verse 9. The first warning is projected into the future and is only hypothetical: "Even if we should preach. . . ." The warning of this verse is stated in the present tense, and points to a situation that is all too real: "If any one is preaching. . . ."

contrary to that which you received — The Galatians were not in doubt as to what Paul was now preaching. The gospel does not change. What they received in the beginning was still true now, and would always be true. The Galatians were perfectly competent to compare for themselves the old gospel with the new. With reference to the gospel it has well been said, "If it's new, it's not true. If it's true, it's not new."

V. 10 **Am I now seeking the favor of men** — Paul was apparently being accused of abandoning the Law to gain the favor of the Gentiles. His opponents probably said Paul lacked the moral fiber and backbone to make the Gentiles toe the mark. They thought they saw in Paul what they often found in themselves — seeking the favor of men, rather than of God. They mistook grace for weakness. (If dogmatism is taking a hard stand on an issue, then what they accused Paul of was "cat-matism" — just pussy-footing around!) Whatever the case, Paul is clearly seen here as a man taking a firm stand on an unpopular issue.

or of God? — There is a dramatic difference between the attitude of false teachers (John 5:44) and the attitude of the apostles (Acts 5:29).

If I were still pleasing men — As Paul says in Phil. 3:4-6, he was at one time a very good lawkeeper. His rapid advancement, however, must have been at least partly due to seeking the praise of men. Popularity is strong wine. Just remember that the Lord said, "Woe to you, when all men speak well of you, for so their father did to the false prophets." (Luke 6:26)

not a servant of Christ — A large percentage of the ancient world was made up of slaves. Through war, poverty, or other misfortune they were forced into involuntary servitude. These people were:
      a. Owned by someone else.
      b. Compelled to do the will of their master.
      c. Deprived of all their rights.
It is a tremendous paradox that Paul should gladly use the very word "slave" (*doulos*) in this epistle of freedom in Christ. It seems folly to those who are perishing, but the only real freedom is in freely chosen servanthood, and the only real victory is in surrender. Jesus himself proved the path of servanthood (Phil. 2:5-8) and Paul willingly followed.

STUDY QUESTIONS:

1. What is an apostle?
2. What word begins and ends each of Paul's epistles, and why is it so important in Galatians?
3. How would you explain the meaning of each of the terms in "Lord Jesus Christ"?
4. How can it be of any value for Jesus to have died for other people's sins?
5. Why was Paul so astonished at the Galatians?

CHAPTER 1 — GALATIANS 1:1-10

6. Why is it a perversion of the gospel to add just a little bit of legalism?
7. What do you do or say when you hear someone distorting the truth of the gospel?
8. Is it possible to please both men and God? (Read Luke 2:52.) Where do you draw the line?
9. What does it mean to be a slave of Christ?

Lesson Two

(1:11-24)

How Paul Became an Apostle (1:11-17)

11 For I would have you know, brethren, that the gospel which was preached by me is not man's gospel. 12 For I did not receive it from man, nor was I taught it, but it came through a revelation of Jesus Christ. 13 For you have heard of my former life in Judaism, how I persecuted the church of God violently and tried to destroy it; 14 and I advanced in Judaism beyond many of my own age among my people, so extemely zealous was I for the traditions of my fathers. 15 But when he who had set me apart before I was born, and had called me through his grace, 16 was pleased to reveal his Son to me, in order that I might preach him among the Gentiles, I did not confer with flesh and blood, 17 nor did I go up to Jerusalem to those who were apostles before me, but I went away into Arabia; and again I returned to Damascus.

Talk about an unlikely prospect for conversion! If ever there was a man who was a hopeless case, it was surely young Saul of Tarsus. In these verses Paul relates his background, conversion, and call to be an apostle. He was neither inclined toward apostleship on his own, nor was he led into it by other men. It was the hand of God.

V. 11 **I would have you know, brethren** — The fact that Paul calls his readers "brethren" is quite significant. Even though they were in the very process of falling from grace (Gal. 5:4), Paul still loves them enough to call them his brothers as he sounds the warning. Eight more times Paul will call them "brethren," including the very last word before his closing "Amen" (6:18).

not man's gospel — The whole point of proving Paul's apostleship was to prove the correctness of his gospel. Paul was not defending a wounded ego or damaged pride. He was confirming the authenticity of the true gospel — for the salvation of their souls! Furthermore, since the gospel Paul preached was from God, the false teachers of Galatia had no right to change it.

V. 12 **I did not receive it from man** — Paul here uses a word which had the special meaning "to receive by oral tradition." Much of the wisdom of ancient times was passed from one generation to the next by skillful oral instruction. Modern critics often say the Scriptures arose by this method as well. Paul says, "Not so!"

nor was I taught it — This refers to the formal teaching of the classroom. Paul had been learning the tenets of Judaism this way at the feet of Gamaliel (Acts 22:3), but this was not the way in which he got the gospel. While we learn the gospel from a human or written source, it was necessary that Paul, as an apostle, get the gospel directly from God.

through a revelation of Jesus Christ — Paul's gospel was true because it was straight from Heaven. The word "revelation" means literally "uncovering" or "unveiling" and is the same term used of the Revelation to John (Rev. 1:1). It usually refers to truth passed from God to man, which man could not discover by his own devices.

V. 13 **my former life in Judaism** — Paul was certainly not proud of his old life, but he mentions it here to prove an important point: He was not sympathetic to the rise of Christianity. His stubborn heart was very much unwilling to believe the reported resurrection. He was not converted because of his softness, but rather in spite of his hardness.

how I persecuted the church of God violently — From the stoning of Stephen (Acts 7:58—8:1) until that day on the Damascus road (Acts 9:1-6), Saul of Tarsus was "breathing threats and murder against the disciples of the Lord." With the zeal of fanaticism, he tried to erase Christianity from the face of the world.

and tried to destroy it — The King James Version says that Paul persecuted the church "and wasted it." The tense of the Greek verb shows that he had not succeeded in destroying the church, but was in the process of trying to do so. Jesus built his church upon the Rock, and the powers of Paul could not prevail against it!

and I advanced in Judaism beyond many of my own age — Paul must have been the star pupil of Gamaliel. It was too bad that he did not exercise the wisdom and restraint of his teacher (Acts 5:34-39). Perhaps

Paul, like many an eager student, hoped to get extra credit for his work outside class. Read Paul's later evaluation of this period in his life in Phil. 3:4-11.

so extremely zealous was I — Paul here uses the same word that was applied to Simon the Zealot (Luke 6:15). The political zealots with whom Simon was associated thought nothing of committing murder to advance their cause. Paul had reached the same point of blind fanaticism. How is it that people can expect to accomplish God's work with the Devil's tools?

the traditions of my fathers — Have you noticed that Paul has referred to his old religious faith three times now, without ever connecting it to God or the Old Covenant? As a matter of fact, the Judaism of Paul's day was so encumbered with human traditions (Mk. 7:8) that it scarcely resembled the covenant given by God at Sinai. Every legal system men have ever had demanded interpretations to guard against the loopholes, and additional rules to guard against the interpretations.

V. 15 **But when he who had set me apart before I was born** — God had plans for Paul before Paul was even born! Paul and his gospel were not "Johnny-come-lately." At just the right time in the sovereign providence of God, Paul was brought into the team of apostles. Please note in this verse two things Paul does not say: first, that God forced him into this plan; or second, that God deals with all people in this same way. God's appointment of Paul as apostle could have been refused or disobeyed (Acts 26:19). Whether God has chosen to operate so directly in every one of our lives is certainly open to discussion. Surely the case of Paul and his apostleship is more special than the average person's choice of vocation.

and had called me through his grace — It must have taken a very special kind of grace for God to throw open his arms of love to a man in the very act of persecuting the church. It is the very nature of God's grace to smile down on people who are in no way deserving of his favor.

V. 16 **was pleased to reveal his Son to me** — The King James Version has a more literal rendering of the Greek: "to reveal his Son *in* me." Probably the intended meaning is best expressed in the New English Bible: "to reveal his Son to me and through me."

that I might preach him among the Gentiles — Paul was God's chosen instrument to carry the gospel to all people, especially the Gentiles (Acts 9:15). Though the legalistic supporters of the Old Testament Law objected, the Jerusalem Christian leaders endorsed and supported Paul in this mission (Gal. 2:9). Paul's urgency in carrying out his commission can be seen in such passages as Rom. 1:15; I Cor. 2:2 and 9:16; Col. 1:28. Even though Paul's great heart yearned for the salvation of his fellow-Jews (Rom. 9:1-5), his preaching was primarily to Gentiles.

CHAPTER 1   GALATIANS 1:18-24

I did not confer with flesh and blood — Following his baptism by Ananias (Acts 9:18) Paul did not seek out Christian teachers to learn the gospel from them. God's plans for him called for a period of three years away from the leaders of the church, as proof that his message was from heaven. The remainder of this chapter proves that Paul was never in a position to obtain his doctrine from other apostles, which would have made his a second-hand gospel.

V. 17 **Nor did I go up to Jerusalem** — The account in Acts 9 confirms that Paul did not go to Jerusalem for a long time after his conversion. When he finally did go to Jerusalem the Christians were afraid to receive him. It even took the encouragement of Barnabas to get the apostles to accept him. Considering Paul's sinister background, their suspicions were understandable.

into Arabia, and again I returned to Damascus — What Paul did in Arabia is not known. Since it is largely desert, he may have gone there for solitude and God's instruction. Since there are also some cities, he may have been preaching. What we do know is that in Damascus he wasted no time, preaching immediately in the synagogues (Acts 9:19-25). The time spent in Arabia may have been a very small part of the three year period mentioned in the next verse.

Paul in Jerusalem (1:18-24)

18 Then after three years I went up to Jerusalem to visit Cephas, and remained with him fifteen days. 19 But I saw none of the other apostles except James the Lord's brother. 20 (In what I am writing to you, before God, I do not lie!) 21 Then I went into the regions of Syria and Cilicia. 22 And I was still not known by sight to the churches of Christ in Judea; 23 they only heard it said, "He who once persecuted us is now preaching the faith he once tried to destroy." 24 And they glorified God because of me.

V. 18 **Then after three years I went up to Jerusalem** — The Jews of Damascus had a fierce hatred toward this star Pharisee who turned Christian. Paul's escape in a basket lowered over the wall is related in Acts 9:23-25. From Damascus he journeyed south to Jerusalem and "went up" the long winding road that climbs to this mountain city.

to visit Cephas — Cephas is the Aramaic equivalent of the Greek name Peter. Both names mean "rock." Paul's reason for this meeting was neither to seek instruction nor to apply for approval. He simply wanted to get acquainted with his fellow apostle.

and remained with him fifteen days — The brevity of this visit proves that Paul got no instruction in Christian doctrine from Peter. The time was simply too short.

V. 19 I saw none of the other apostles — Either the other apostles were preaching elsewhere, or they were not so bold as the big fisherman to meet their former enemy. The important point here in Galatians is how little contact Paul had with other apostles.

except James the Lord's brother — During the earthly ministry of Jesus, James had been an unbeliever (John 7:5). After meeting the risen Lord (I Cor. 15:7) James became an important leader in the Jerusalem church (Acts 15:13-21). So far as history records, he was never appointed apostle. The following paraphrase, which fits the Greek perfectly well, is the probable solution: "I saw none of the other apostles, but I did see James the Lord's brother. (I mention him because he is also a leader of importance.)"

Do not forget that the whole thrust of this passage is how little contact Paul had with the apostles. They had received their gospel first-hand from Jesus, and so had Paul.

V. 20 (In what I am writing to you, before God, I do not lie!) — Paul has sworn to tell the truth, the whole truth, and nothing but the truth before the court of his readers' judgment. The base accusations of the Judaizers evoked from Paul this unusually strong pronouncement of his truthfulness. The facts of his earlier life were points of evidence to prove the non-human origin of his gospel.

V. 21 Then I went into the regions of Syria and Cilicia — After spending two weeks with the Christians in Jerusalem, Paul was sent on to his home town of Tarsus (in Cilicia) as Luke relates in Acts 10:30. Some time later Barnabas took Paul back to Antioch (in Syria) to help in the work among the Greek-speaking people. Paul continued in this work for a whole year, teaching a large company of believers. It was here in Antioch that believers first came to be called "Christians" (Acts 11:25-26).

V. 22 And I was still not known by sight — The many congregations spread throughout Judea still did not know Paul by sight (literally "by face"). By the time most of the province heard of his arrival, he was already gone. The quick, temporary nature of the visit is underscored.

V. 23 They only heard it said — Imagine the surprise and wonder of the early Christians when the rumors from distant Damascus were confirmed by first-hand reports from Jerusalem! What they had not yet seen for themselves became the topic of all their conversations.

"He who once persecuted us is now preaching the faith — Many had persecuted the early Christians, but none with the zeal of Paul. Now that he was converted, he was preaching with a zeal few could match. What Paul preached was "the faith," which here designates the gospel message (Jude 3). The word for preaching is actually "evangelizing," the Greek word for the joyous shout of the king's herald who has good news to tell.

he once tried to destroy" — The King James Version has "the faith which

CHAPTER 1   GALATIANS 1:18-24

once he destroyed." As in verse 13, the better translation would show that Paul did not succeed in what he was attempting.

V. 24 **And they glorified God because of me** — It would have been quite human to resent Paul's conversion and forgiveness of all past sin. But the Christians rejoiced and glorified God. Once they accepted him, it would also have been quite human to lionize him, making a great public show of their important new convert. Such a terrible sinner's testimony would make an exciting program! However, they did not glorify and make much of Paul — they glorified God.

Paul was not seeking their favor. If he had been, he would no longer have been the slave of Christ (Gal. 1:10). Paul boasted of neither his former sin, nor his present conversion. He preached Christ and the people glorified God.

STUDY QUESTIONS:

1. Why does Paul take so much space to remind his readers of how he became a Christian and an apostle?
2. What is important about the use of the word "brethren" in verse 11?
3. Describe young Saul as a star pupil of Gamaliel.
4. Does sincere zeal make up for being on the wrong side?
5. Did God set us apart for anything before we were born?
6. What did Paul do immediately after his conversion?
7. Why did Paul go to Jerusalem, and whom did he see there?
8. Why mention James the Lord's brother?
9. Was Paul wrong to have sworn with the formal oath form in verse 20?
10. What did Paul do in Syria and Cilicia?
11. What is the best response to gospel preaching?

Lesson Three

(2:1-10)

The Jerusalem Council (2:1-5)
1 Then after fourteen years I went up again to Jerusalem with Barnabas, taking Titus along with me. 2 I went up by revelation; and I laid before them (but privately before those who were of repute) the gospel which I preach among the Gentiles, lest somehow I should be running or had run in vain. 3 But even Titus, who was with me, was not compelled to be circumcised, though he was a Greek. 4 But because of false brethren secretly brought in, who slipped in to spy out our freedom which we have in Christ Jesus, that they might bring us into bondage — 5 to them we did not yield submission even for a moment, that the truth of the gospel might be preserved for you.

At last, the showdown! Back in Jerusalem where it all began, the great question would be settled: Must a Christian first of all keep the Old Testament law? The legalists were prepared to gun down Paul and his gospel of freedom. Paul was prepared to lay before everyone what God had been doing through him among the Gentiles. The other apostles were prepared to listen and discern the will of God in the matter.

V. 1 **After fourteen years I went up again to Jerusalem** — During this space of fourteen years Paul and Barnabas first labored in the church in Antioch. Then, at the prompting of the Holy Spirit, they were sent out

CHAPTER 2   GALATIANS 2:1-5

on what we call the First Missionary Journey. On this journey they passed through the cities of Antioch of Pisidia, Iconium, Lystra, and Derbe, making Christians and establishing churches. This area was called Galatia on Roman maps. Probably some of the very readers of this epistle became Christians because of this First Missionary Journey.

A careful reading of Acts, however, discloses another visit to Jerusalem by Paul (Acts 11:30). Why is there no mention of this trip in Galatians? (Certain critics, as one might expect, charge that the author is here guilty of either error or outright deception.) Surely the correct view is simply that Paul omitted mention of this trip because it was not relevant to the issue. This trip to Jerusalem had nothing to do with Paul's gospel or his apostleship. They were making delivery of money for famine relief, and that was all. If Paul had detailed everything he did during this fourteen year period, the epistle to the Galatians would have been very much longer!

with Barnabas, taking Titus along — Barnabas had been a fellow-preacher with Paul, and went more or less as an equal. Titus was one of several helpers, and was taken along not as a preacher of equal standing, but as a case in point. Titus was a Greek, not a Jew, and had never been circumcised. Would he now, as a Christian, have to submit to this legal rite in order to be acceptable to God?

V. 2 **I went up by revelation** — Paul himself felt no compelling need to obtain the approval of the Jerusalem apostles. He knew his gospel was from God, and that was enough. However, it must have seemed better in heaven's wisdom to bring all the leaders together and have them take a united stand on this issue. When the will of God on this meeting was revealed, Paul and Barnabas were appointed by the church in Antioch to go to Jerusalem (Acts 15:1-4).

I laid before them (but privately before those who were of repute) — Simple courtesy and common decency demanded that Paul first meet privately with the other leaders and discuss the issue with them. Little would be gained by waiting for a public confrontation and then dropping the matter on them like a bombshell. Paul was certainly not overawed by their rank or importance (see also verse 6), but he did want to be fair and give them a chance to perceive the truth of the matter. Paul approached them with the attitude of a man who has nothing to fear from a close inspection and thorough testing.

lest somehow I should be running or had run in vain — Even if the decision of the leaders had gone against Paul, it would not have proved Paul wrong. He was right, and he knew it! "Running in vain" does not refer to the chance that his gospel was wrong, but to the possibility that the Jew-Gentile unity he had labored to achieve would be destroyed.

V. 3 **Titus ... was not compelled to be circumcised** — The agreement that Gentile Christians like Titus did not need the rite of circumcision freed them from the whole burden of the old covenant. This landmark case carried with it two important corollaries. First, women could now enter into the covenant relationship with God on an equal basis with men. They had been physically ineligible for circumcision under the old covenant and were considered to be inferior, but now in Christ "there is neither male nor female." (Gal. 3:28) Second, the whole system of legalism was dealt a death blow. The self-righteous law-keepers could no longer boast. Salvation was a free gift of God to all who would humbly accept it through faith in Jesus Christ.

though he was a Greek — Paul could have easily left Titus at home to avoid any controversy, but he wanted to bring the problem to a head. Since Titus was present, it was no mere theological debate. It was a very practical question, and one that could not be left hanging: Must Titus be circumcised, or not?

V. 4 **false brethren secretly brought in** — Certain men were only pretending to belong to Christ. They were "pseudo" brothers, who had smuggled themselves in. In an interesting parallel the Greek historian Strabo wrote of the enemies of a city who were "secretly brought in" by traitors within. The Judaizers in Jerusalem were false in their pretentions and were lying about their aims.

who slipped in to spy out our freedom — The Judaizers were envious of the happy freedom the Gentile Christians had. They infiltrated the conference, hoping somehow to lay bare and destroy this freedom. No Christian, thought the Judaizers, had any right to be so free and happy! The ironic point of it all was this: The Judaizers could be just as free from legalism and just as happy in Christ themselves. They did not want to have this freedom, however; they just wanted to deprive others of it.

that they might bring us into bondage — To add legalism to the Christian system is literally to "enslave" the believers. The intensive word used here by Paul means "to break the spirit of someone, and reduce him to slavery."

V. 5 **we did not yield submission even for a moment** — Paul, who became all things to all people (I Cor. 9:22), would not budge an inch on this issue. While he would gladly compromise on cultural matters, and give up his rights to protect a weaker brother (I Cor. 8:13), Paul refused to yield in any way to the principle of legalism. Legalism is like crabgrass — once it gets a foothold, it just keeps growing and spreading until it takes over completely.

How does this apply to us today? When should we give in and when should we stand our ground with the brother who objects to eating in the church basement, or to wearing blue jeans in worship, or to playing the piano? If we are dealing with a weaker brother who is in danger of losing his faith, we should be prepared to give up our rights. If we are dealing with a would-be dictator who is in danger of losing only his temper, we should stand our ground to preserve the truth of the gospel's freedom.

that the truth of the gospel might be preserved for you — Two things should be observed about Paul's stand. He was defending a principle of Christian freedom, not a personal privilege. And he was doing it for others, not for himself.

The Right Hand of Fellowship (2:6-10)

6 And from those who were reputed to be something (what they were makes no difference to me; God shows no partiality) — those, I say, who were of repute added nothing to me; 7 but on the contrary, when they saw that I had been entrusted with the gospel to the uncircumcised, just as Peter had been entrusted with the gospel to the circumcised 8 (for he who worked through Peter for the mission to the circumcised worked through me also for the Gentiles), 9 and when they perceived the grace that was given to me, James and Cephas and John, who were reputed to be pillars, gave to me and Barnabas the right hand of fellowship, that we should go to the Gentiles and they to the circumcised; 10 only they would have us remember the poor, which very thing I was eager to do.

V. 6 **Those who were reputed to be something** — Paul cared little about a man's reputation, what a man is reputed to be. While some people may have tried to treat James, Cephas, and John like "Big Shots," Paul did not. In speaking this way Paul was not belittling the leaders. Rather, he was rejecting human appraisals.

(what they were makes no difference to me — Paul showed an admirable balance in his approach. He showed the proper respect for leadership by meeting first with them privately, but also showed that he was not overawed by their position. Lesser men tend to fall from this balance, either stooping and bowing to lick the boots of leaders, or treating them with contempt.

God shows no partiality) — God is not impressed by a man's office or reputation. The original Greek phrase says, "God does not take a man's face." He is neither impressed nor influenced by reputation, wealth (James 2:1), or nationality (Rom. 2:11). God is like the idealized statue of justice which is blindfolded, so that the verdict of law will not be determined by things such as "Jew or Greek, slave or free, male or female." (See Gal. 3:28.)

who were of repute added nothing to me — Here is the main point of these verses: The Jerusalem apostles found no defect in Paul's gospel. It was the same gospel they had received from the Lord. Nothing needed to be added (such as circumcision), and nothing could be taken away.

V. 7 **But on the contrary, when they saw** — The only changing of position was done by the "pillars." Paul left the conference preaching the same gospel he had come with. It was the leaders who gained new insight into God's plan.

I had been entrusted — The deciding factor in the decision of the apostles was not that they liked Paul, or liked his gospel. The critical truth was that the gospel had come from God. To Paul, as a faithful steward (I Cor. 4:1-2), the sacred message had been entrusted. The only right basis for judgment was this: Is it from God?

gospel to the uncircumcised — As noted previously, Paul never preached exclusively to the Gentiles. It was only after the Jews rejected him in each city that he sadly excluded them from his work. Likewise in the case of Peter, there was occasional crossing of ethnic lines, as in the conversion of Cornelius (Acts 10 and 11). Nevertheless, it was God's strategy to send Paul to Gentiles, and Peter to Jews, and this was seen to be good by the conference.

V. 8 **(for he who worked** — It was God who was working in (literally "energizing") both Peter and Paul. They wisely recognized that both their ministries were equally valid in God's kingdom. Neither disparaged the other for being sent in a different direction.

V. 9 **the grace that was given to me** — Paul did not mean by this that he now possessed a quantity of magical grace to be dispensed on the heads of those who kneel before him. What he had been given was a job, a mission. This was "the grace that was given" to him. (See also Eph. 3:1-7). Here, as always, the free gift of God's grace carries with it the idea of a response and a responsibility (See Eph. 2:8 and 10).

James and Cephas and John, who were reputed to be pillars — This is James the Lord's brother (Gal. 1:18), not James the son of Zebedee, who had been killed by Herod (Acts 12:2). It was common in the ancient world to refer to proved and trustworthy men as "pillars." The pillar is a main supporting part of a structure, just as is the foundation (Eph. 2:20).

gave to me and Barnabas — Paul and Barnabas were the two preachers of the First Missionary Journey (Acts 13:2ff.) They represented the gospel's evangelistic thrust among the Gentiles. Even after they no longer traveled as a team, both preached God's grace to Gentiles (Acts 15:36-41).

the right hand of fellowship — The Greek word *koinonia* means a state of sharing or partnership. It is even used frequently of marriage, the most intimate of human relationships. In its general use in scripture it refers to the life which all Christians have in common in Christ. We share this life with God and Jesus, and we also share it with one another (I John 1:3). In this sense of the word, it is not necessary that a Christian endorse every action or opinion of his brother to have fellowship with him. The mere fact that they both are sons of God brings them together in the same family.

In this passage, however, fellowship seems to have a special meaning. When the apostles extended the right hand of fellowship to Paul and Barnabas they were accepting them as partners. What is more, they were accepting, approving, and endorsing the gospel which Paul and Barnabas were preaching. This formal stamp of approval on their work is something more than the general fellowship among Christian people.

It should be noted that Paul did not go to Jerusalem as a subordinate seeking the approval of his superiors. He went, and was accepted, as an apostle among apostles. These leaders all recognized their equal roles on God's team.

V. 10 **Only they would have us remember the poor** — The saints in Judea were still suffering the effects of widespread famine (Acts 11:27-30). Paul and Barnabas had already brought contributions at least once before (Acts 11:30), and Paul would continue to gather funds for this cause (as in II Cor. 8:1 — 9:15).

which very thing I was eager to do — The separation of Paul and Peter in their labors certainly did not mean that the Gentile Christians were separated from Jewish Christians. They realized that they were fellow-members of God's household (Eph. 2:19), and were eager to use any opportunity to assist one another (Gal. 6:10).

STUDY QUESTIONS:

1. Why did Paul take Titus along?
2. Why was circumcision such an important issue?
3. Why did Paul meet the leaders privately?
4. How does Acts 15 describe the "false brethren" who opposed Paul at the Jerusalem Council?
5. What was Paul's attitude toward "those of repute"?
6. Explain the literal meaning of "God shows no partiality."
7. How did Cephas (Peter) contribute to the Council in Acts 15?
8. What was the conclusion of James in Acts 15?
9. What is meant by "grace" in verse nine?
10. Explain the "right hand of fellowship."
11. Why should the leaders have considered it necessary to ask that Paul and the Gentiles "remember the poor"?

Lesson Four

(2:11-21)

Paul Opposes Cephas (2:11-14)

11 But when Cephas came to Antioch I opposed him to his face, because he stood condemned. 12 For before certain men came from James, he ate with the Gentiles; but when they came he drew back and separated himself, fearing the circumcision party. 13 And with him the rest of the Jews acted insincerely, so that even Barnabas was carried away by their insincerity. 14 But when I saw that they were not straightforward about the truth of the gospel, I said to Cephas before them all, "If you, though a Jew, live like a Gentile and not like a Jew, how can you compel the Gentiles to live like Jews?"

Another showdown! Paul had successfully defended the gospel against false brethren in Jerusalem, but now he faced a fellow-apostle in Antioch. The opponent this time was perhaps more sincere, but he was still wrong. So, Paul met the problem head-on. God's gospel is true, though every man a liar — even if that man is the apostle Peter!

V. 11 When Cephas came to Antioch — Some time after the Jerusalem Council, Cephas (Peter — see notes on 1:18) went to Antioch to visit Paul and the Gentile Christians. The visit is not recorded in Acts, so all we know about it are the few details given in this text.

I opposed him to his face — Peter made a glaring error, as is explained

CHAPTER 2   GALATIANS 2:11-14

in the next verse. Paul could have attacked Peter behind his back, but he chose to confront him face to face. This is the only right way to oppose a brother.

because he stood condemned — In refusing to be seen eating with Gentiles, Peter violated what he surely knew was right. Both the decree of God in Acts 10:15 and the decision of the Council in Acts 15:28-29 clearly condone the diet of the Gentiles. When Peter stopped eating with the Gentiles, he was wrong and he knew it.

V. 12 **Before certain men came from James** — The text does not state that these men had been sent from James with any sinister motives. For whatever reason they had been sent, their arrival surprised Peter in the act of eating with the Gentiles. Caught off guard and embarrassed, Peter quickly abandoned his non-Jewish friends.

he ate with the Gentiles — While the Gentile Christians had been pronounced free from the law, the Jewish Christians were unsure about their own state. Peter should be commended for going beyond the letter of the law and following the spirit of the Jerusalem decree. He rightly surmised that God was also freeing the Jews from the legalistic burden. In the spirit of Christian liberty Peter sat, for the first time in his life, at a Gentile table.

but when they came — With the sudden arrival of Jewish Christians from Jerusalem, Peter was no longer certain about his right to eat Gentile food. Like a criminal caught in the act of committing a crime, Peter hastily withdrew.

he drew back and separated himself — Peter strained at the gnat and swallowed the camel (Matt. 23:24). To avoid a possible ceremonial contamination with what was "unclean," he committed a very grievous sin before God. He set aside brothers for whom Christ died.

When the text says Peter "drew back" it uses the word which means to "shrink back from something repulsive, as in fear or disgust." Suddenly the Gentile Christians were as unwelcome as lepers! When Peter "separated" himself, he was completely cutting himself off from these brothers. In effect, he was excommunicating them. Perhaps the Gentile Christians could take comfort in the words of Jesus when he used the same term, "Happy are you when men shall hate you and *reject you.*" It was a bitter pill to swallow, however, that this rejection came from a fellow Christian — even an apostle!

fearing the circumcision party — The old Peter, who had denied his Lord before a little girl, was coming to the surface. Although he had already decided that eating with Gentiles was right in the sight of God, he was worried how it might look in the sight of men. No doubt the Jerusalem Christians were a bit surprised to find Peter "defiling" himself, but their surprise should not have mattered. Peter simply lacked the courage of his convictions.

V. 13 **the rest of the Jews acted insincerely** — Peter had set the example for the other Jewish-Christians. Together they acted insincerely (literally, "played the hypocrite together"). The word "hypocrite" came from the Greek theater, where actors wore the masks of comedy or tragedy, and were called "play-actors." The outward appearance and actions of an actor are not the same as his inner nature. In Peter's situation his inner Christ-likeness was not being matched by his actions.

even Barnabas was carried away — It is ironic that brave Barnabas, who had championed the underdog in Acts 9:27, should now desert the Gentile Christians. It is ironic, even shocking, to find the co-leader of the first great missionary journey to the Gentiles (Acts 13:2ff.) now joining the action against them. (It makes one wonder if this could have contributed to the parting of ways between Paul and Barnabas in Acts 15:36-39.)

V. 14 **When I saw that they were not straightforward** — To be straightforward means "to walk in a straight line." Peter and the brethren were out of line with the decision of the Jerusalem Council, and more than that, out of line with the decree of God. The gospel allows no such discrimination.

the truth of the gospel — Paul had much more in mind than church socials when he included this incident in our epistle. The whole point of this section is this: Can one man and the true gospel stand against Peter, Barnabas, and the whole group of important visitors from Jerusalem? This passage draws a clear conclusion: one man, standing squarely on the truth of the gospel, constitutes a majority.

I said to Cephas before them all — Why did Paul rebuke Peter so publicly? Why not rebuke him in private? Peter's sin was a public sin, with consequences involving many people. Such a public sin required a public correction. The whole question of Jew and Gentile fellowship was at stake.

"If you, though a Jew, live like a Gentile — Peter had begun to realize that Christ had set him free from certain Jewish rituals and ceremonies. He was cautiously leaving them behind. Now, in a sudden turnabout, he has insisted that the Gentiles be more Jewish than he himself. Peter surely realized his glaring inconsistency.

Just how much of the Mosaic law and customs the Jewish Christians were keeping is hard to determine. As late as Acts 21:20-26, they were still making vows in the temple. With the destruction of the temple in 70 A.D. God's final verdict on Jewish practices was made clear.

CHAPTER 2　　　　　　　　　　　　　　　　　GALATIANS 2:15-21

Justified by Faith in Christ (2:15-21)

15 We ourselves, who are Jews by birth and not Gentile sinners, 16 yet who know that a man is not justified by works of the law but through faith in Jesus Christ, even we have believed in Christ Jesus, in order to be justified by faith in Christ, and not by works of the law, because by works of the law shall no one be justified. 17 But if, in our endeavor to be justified in Christ, we ourselves were found to be sinners, is Christ then an agent of sin? Certainly not! 18 But if I build up again those things which I tore down, then I prove myself a transgressor. 19 For I through the law died to the law, that I might live to God. 20 I have been crucified with Christ; it is no longer I who live, but Christ who lives in me; and the life I now live in the flesh I live by faith in the Son of God, who loved me and gave himself for me. 21 I do not nullify the grace of God; for if justification were through the law, then Christ died to no purpose.

V. 15 **Jews by birth and not Gentile sinners** — "Gentile sinners," as they were typically called by the Jews, might have objected to keeping dietary laws for purely selfish reasons. "Jews by birth," such as Paul and Peter, now must also see that such regulations have been abolished.

V. 16 **yet who know** — Both Peter and Paul knew this truth of the gospel. Paul was not forcing a strange new doctrine on Peter; he was urging him to face up to what he already knew.

a man is not justified by works of the law — This is the grand gospel truth. Man is not justified by keeping the law. In fact, man is free not only from the Old Testament law, but from any law. The Greek text, as Paul wrote it, does not have the word "the" before law. Therefore, man is free from law — not just from the law (of Moses). While it was the Mosaic law that the people knew best, it was not just that law that was cancelled. All legalism is dead!

Paul spoke similarly of "law" and not just "the law" in Gal. 2:19; 3:2, 5, and 10. This is clearly stated in Romans 3:21 as well: "But now the righteousness of God has been manifested apart from *law*, although *the law* and the prophets bear witness to it."

but through faith in Jesus Christ — When Martin Luther rediscovered this glorious truth, the Protestant Reformation began, and the shackles of Roman Catholicism were broken. It is by faith, not by works of law, that a man is justified or pronounced innocent before God. Now the kind of faith that thus justifies is active (James 2:17) and energetic (Gal. 5:6). Let no man pretend to have this faith who merely believes a few facts about Jesus. Real faith is commitment and trust. He who truly commits himself to Jesus and trusts him as Lord is counted as righteous by God.

even we have believed in Christ Jesus — "We," Paul and Peter, have put our commitment and trust in Jesus.

in order to be justified — To be justified is to be pronounced innocent and acquitted. It is not to escape punishment on a mere technicality and then walk through the rest of life branded as a criminal who slipped past justice. It is to be able to stand before God clean and pure, "just-as-if-I'd" never sinned.

because by works of the law shall no one be justified — Again, what Paul actually said was "by works of law." He did not say "the law." Just as David wrote in Psalm 143:2, no man can earn his way into a state of righteousness before God.

V. 17 **But if, in our endeavor** — Paul now moves to meet two possible problems in the doctrine of salvation by faith in Christ. Verse seventeen presents the first possible hazard, and verse eighteen presents the second. Let me explain them in this way:

(vs. 17) What if I tear down all law, and then abuse my freedom and become very sinful?

(vs. 18) What if, on the other hand, I build the law back and then try to obey it?

As we analyze the first possible hazard, we must admit that it is certainly possible for a man to abuse his freedom. But if he does, it is not Christ's fault. (Certainly not!, or God forbid! — KJV) Just as when any child grows up, God's children are given freedom as mature sons in Christ. Whether the new freedom leads on to sin or to righteousness depends on the person's heart. Yes! There is some danger involved in giving the new adult his freedom. But — the only alternative to liberty is law . . . and permanent guardianship.

As we analyze the second hazard, we must admit that it is possible for someone to try to go back and keep the law of Moses, or perhaps some other legal code. However, the very best that such a person could hope for is to prove all over again that he is a transgressor and cannot keep all the laws.

Between the extremes of lawless chaos and legal chains is the position of the Christian. His life is being molded by the will of his Lord and his actions are motivated by love. God's precepts become the principles by which he lives, and he follows the high ethical standards because he wants to, not because he has to.

V. 19 **For I through the law died to the law** — Law was a very harsh taskmaster. It burdened and beat Paul (as well as all men) until they collapsed under the load. Law made demands, but gave no ability to meet those demands. All the law could do was demand, forbid, judge, condemn. Finally Paul, as the slave of the law, was beaten to death.

that I might live to God — Law can only kill; only God can make alive. Now that Paul has been brought back to life in Christ, he is free to live for Christ.

CHAPTER 2   GALATIANS 2:15-21

V. 20 **I have been crucified with Christ** — Law demanded death as the penalty for sin (Ezekiel 18:10). When Christ went to the cross to pay that penalty, Paul went with him. In fact, every Christian was there, dying and paying the price for sin, in the person of Jesus Christ.

it is no longer I who live, but Christ who lives in me — The old man of sin is dead. The new man has been made alive by the spirit of Christ. Freed from the shackles and chains of the former master, the Christian is open under new management. He has denied self (Matt. 16:24-25) and has yielded to the entry of a new spirit (Rom. 8:9). He can say with Paul in Phil. 1:21 that "to live is Christ."

the life I now live in the flesh — On the surface it might seem that men killed by the law and made alive by God just go on living the same as before. While they do remain on earth and in their bodies, however, they have a new spirit and their citizenship is in heaven (Phil. 3:20).

I live by faith in the Son of God — Faith in Christ becomes the motivating principle for all of life. If any man should abandon Christ as the reason and purpose for his living, he would of course revert to a standing before God based on law. (See Gal. 5:1-6).

who loved me and gave himself for me — The price paid at Calvary makes possible freedom from legalism. When Jesus has done so much for us, is it not reasonable that we should gladly live by our commitment of faith in him?

V. 21 **I do not nullify the grace of God** — The way Paul could have nullified God's grace was by choosing legalism. When God tried to give salvation as a gift, Paul could have said, "No thanks! I don't need your charity. I'm going to earn this all by myself."

if justification were through the law, then Christ died to no purpose — Christ did not die just to give us a better way or an easier way. He died on Calvary because that was the only way!

STUDY QUESTIONS:

1. How did Paul correct Peter? (See vs. 11 and 14.) Why was this the right way to do it?
2. Why did Peter stop eating with the Gentiles?
3. What was the reaction of Barnabas?
4. Did Jews who became Christians continue to keep such rules as the diet laws? (See vs. 14.)
5. Why did Paul say "Gentile sinners" in verse 15?
6. What is the difference between "works of law" and "works of the law"?

THIRTEEN LESSONS ON GALATIANS

7. What does it mean to be justified?
8. What are the dangers of discontinuing the law? (See vs. 17 and 18.)
9. In what way is the Christian "crucified with Christ"?
10. How might a person nullify God's grace?

Lesson Five

(3:1-14)

By Works or By Faith? (3:1-5)
1 O foolish Galatians! Who has bewitched you, before whose eyes Jesus Christ was publicly portrayed as crucified? 2 Let me ask you only this: Did you receive the Spirit by works of the law, or by hearing with faith? 3 Are you so foolish? Having begun with the Spirit, are you now ending with the flesh? 4 Did you experience so many things in vain? — if it really is in vain. 5 Does he who supplies the Spirit to you and works miracles among you do so by works of the law, or by hearing with faith?

Using the skill of an attorney, Paul now begins the point-by-point argument section of his epistle. For two chapters Paul will pile up argument upon argument to prove that we are saved by grace, not by works of law. He will argue from Scripture, from experience, from illustrations in everyday life, and even from allegory. The force of all this is nothing short of overwhelming, to any who are willing to listen and reason.

V. 1   **O foolish Galatians!** — In a sharp style much like verse six of chapter one, Paul calls the Galatians "mindless."

Who has bewitched you — Paul used a word from the field of magic and superstition, in calling them "bewitched." The popular belief held that the "evil eye" could cast some sort of spell on people to make them act strangely. Paul, of course, does not hold the superstition, but he is

THIRTEEN LESSONS ON GALATIANS

using the word's association with ignorant superstition to shame them. He says, in effect, "Surely you were not in your right mind when you decided to give up on Jesus and his sacrifice for you!"

before whose eyes Jesus Christ was publicly portrayed as crucified — The Galatians were not in Jerusalem when Jesus was crucified, but Paul's preaching was so vivid and clear that they could virtually see the whole drama unfolding. Just as in Corinth, Paul preached "Christ crucified" (I Cor. 1:23 and 2:2).

In secular Greek usage the word for "publicly portrayed" was used for official notices and public proclamations. It had much the sense of posting on a billboard for all to see.

V. 2 **Let me ask you only this** — Here begins the first of seven arguments which make up chapter three. These arguments may be summarized in this way:

(1) Law or faith: which gave you the Spirit? (vs. 2-5)
(2) Law or faith: which makes sons of Abraham? (vs. 6-9)
(3) Law or faith: which promises a curse? (vs. 10-14)
(4) Example of a man's will (vs. 15-18)
(5) Why was the law given, anyway? (vs. 19-20)
(6) Is the law competing against the promises? (vs. 21-22)
(7) Only a custodian (vs. 23-26)

Did you receive the Spirit by works of the law? — Paul appeals to his readers' own experience. Did they receive the Holy Spirit when they kept God's laws or when they accepted Christ? The answer was obvious. In the Old Testament the Spirit of the Lord came upon selected individuals, for only a short period of time, as in the example of Samson (Judges 14:6, 14:19, and 15:14). The day was yet to come when the Spirit would be poured out on all flesh (Joel 2:28) to dwell within God's child as a permanent resident.

V. 3 **Are you so foolish?** — As in verse one, the word "foolish" means mindless or unthinking.

Having begun with the Spirit — Since they began the Spiritual life in Christ, what could be gained by going back to the law? They would be reversing God's plan, and moving backwards from spiritual maturity to infancy.

V. 4 **Did you experience so many things in vain?** — Was it for nothing that God had poured out his Spirit and blessings on them? Would they look at all this and then walk away?

The word "experience" may also be translated "suffer," as in the KJV. If this is what Paul meant, then he was referring to past persecutions and hardships. Having gone through so much, would they now give it up so easily?

CHAPTER 3   GALATIANS 3:6-9

if it really is in vain — Even in the middle of a rebuke, Paul still is hopeful for the future of his Galatian converts. Whether that hope is justified, or it has all been in vain, is up to the Galatians themselves.

V. 5 **he who supplies the Spirit to you and works miracles** — The coming of the Spirit to the Galatians was made visible by the working of miracles. It was a frequent occurrence in the early church for signs and wonders to accompany the preaching of the apostles (Heb. 2:3-4). The purpose of the miracles was to confirm what they proclaimed as true. By this proof of the Spirit's presence the Galatians could decide if faith in Christ was right. The confirming miracles ceased to be given when the infant church reached maturity, with the written New Testament replacing the physical presence of the apostles.

Sons of Abraham (3:6-9)

6 Thus Abraham "believed God, and it was reckoned to him as righteousness." 7 So you see that it is men of faith who are the sons of Abraham. 8 And the scripture, foreseeing that God would justify the Gentiles by faith, preached the gospel beforehand to Abraham, saying, "In you shall all the nations be blessed." 9 So then, those who are men of faith are blessed with Abraham who had faith.

V. 6 **Thus Abraham** — Paul's second argument is based on how a person becomes a son of Abraham. The Judaizers had probably taught that one must join Abraham in circumcision to share in the promised blessings. Paul will show, however, that Abraham is father of those who have faith, not those who are circumcised.

"believed God, and it was reckoned to him as righteousness" — Abraham found favor in God's eyes because of his faith. And, as Paul clearly points out in Rom. 4:10, this happened before Abraham was circumcised! When the scripture says in Gen. 15:6 that his faith was "reckoned" as righteousness, it uses a common accounting term which meant "to credit to one's account."

V. 7 **So you see** — It must be obvious to any fair-minded person that if we want to join Abraham in God's favor, we must do it through faith instead of circumcision, just as Abraham did.

V. 8 **And the scripture, foreseeing** — Here the scripture is treated almost as a living, thinking thing. The idea behind these words is probably that the Holy Spirit, who authored the scripture, foresaw what was coming.

that God would justify the Gentiles by faith — God's plan has not changed. The gospel of grace through Jesus Christ was the intended means of salvation from the very beginning. This thought will be developed further in verses 15 to 17.

preached the gospel beforehand to Abraham — The "good news" of the coming Saviour was included in compact form in the promises to Abraham. Few details were given, but there was enough substance for people to put their faith in.

"In you shall all the nations be blessed." — The promise was first made to Abraham in Gen. 12:1-3 and is repeated several times in similar words (15:5; 17:4-5; 18:18; 22:17). The Jews thought that the Gentiles would first have to be circumcised to become Abraham's sons. God had other plans.

V. 9 **So then, those who are men of faith** — It is clear from Paul's argument, that we become partners with Abraham by joining him in his kind of faith. It might be well to remind ourselves what kind of faith that was.

blessed with Abraham who had faith — The fulfillment of God's promise of blessing all nations is made possible through faith. Men do not have to become Jews first. Men of any nationality may approach God on the same basis as Abraham — faith. Furthermore, the promise is only to those of all nations who do have this faith. All men, of whatever nation, who do not have faith are condemned (John 3:18).

The Curse of the Law (3:10-14)

10 For all who rely on works of the law are under a curse; for it is written, "Cursed be every one who does not abide by all things written in the book of the law, and do them." 11 Now it is evident that no man is justified before God by the law; for "He who through faith is righteous shall live"; 12 but the law does not rest on faith, for "He who does them shall live by them." 13 Christ redeemed us from the curse of the law, having become a curse for us — for it is written, "Cursed be every one who hangs on a tree" — 14 that in Christ Jesus the blessing of Abraham might come upon the Gentiles, that we might receive the promise of the Spirit through faith.

V. 10 **For all who rely on works of the law** — Just as in 2:16, Paul omits the definite article and says simply "works of law." All people who approach God on the basis of legalism are in trouble, regardless of which legal code or law they have tried to keep. The specific failure of the Jews and the Mosaic Law is typical of all men and all legal codes. If anyone tries to make a lawbook out of the New Testament they will likewise fail to live up to its demands.

are under a curse — The Old Testament itself will provide proof of the constant peril of those who try to justify themselves before God by works of law. The curse is promised within the Law itself.

for it is written — Just as Moses charged the people in Deut. 27:26, the man who does not do what the law says is accursed. To this the people replied, "Amen." Paul adds the word "all" to make it even more emphatic that anyone who fails to keep any commandment of the law is doomed. This is the promise of the law!

V. 11 Now it is evident — Paul now brings in a scripture statement from Hab. 2:4 to clinch his argument. Here God has clearly said that those who are justified *by faith* will live. While the Law brought constant peril, faith brings constant promise.

The Law: "Do it all, or die!"
Faith: "Believe in me, and live!"

Every man must choose the avenue by which he approaches God. He can choose the peril of legalism or the promise of faith, but not both at the same time.

V. 12 But the law does not rest on faith — It is necessary to show that law and faith are not compatible. God promised to give justification to those who have faith, but the Law says they have to earn it. Thus the Law is not content to stand on the promises, but rushes out to attain self-justification.

"He who does them shall live by them." — This passage from Lev. 18:5 points out the requirement of the Law. Despite the promise that "He who through faith is righteous shall live," the Law says the only way to live is by doing the works.

V. 13 Christ redeemed us from the curse of the law — All men under law are under a curse. This was especially true of the Jews, who had the most complete revelation of God's law. With all mankind in this predicament, Jesus came to our rescue! Men were trapped under the law's curse by their own admitted inability to keep all the law. So, just like the man who purchases the freedom of a slave, Christ "redeemed" us. The word "redeemed" actually means "to buy or buy back, at personal expense." The Law demanded death as the penalty for our sins, and Christ offered himself as the payment.

having become a curse for us — The only one who had never known sin in himself was made to be sin for our sake (II Cor. 5:21). The Old Testament also supports the association of Christ's death with the curse, in the text from Deut. 21:23, which Paul here quotes. It is also in the light of this curse that we should understand God turning away from his Son during the climax of the crucifixion (Matt. 27:46). The awfulness of that physical death was far surpassed by death of spiritual separation. Such was the cost of Calvary.

"Cursed by every one who hangs on a tree" — The practice of crucifixion was not Jewish. However, the Jews did take the bodies of executed criminals and hang them on trees as a mark of public shame. The grisly spectacle of nailing the living to a stake or cross, and then watching them

CHAPTER 3 GALATIANS 3:10-14

die, was yet to be developed after the time of Moses and Deut. 21:23.

Crucifixion in ancient Greece and Carthage was done on a simple wooden stake. Later crucifixion added the cross beam. The Romans adopted this form of crucifixion, using it only in the punishment of slaves for very serious crimes. It was the supposed treason of Jesus against the state of Rome which made him eligible for this death. (See John 19:12-16.)

V. 14 **That in Christ Jesus** — This is a purpose phrase, indicating the purpose of the cross.

the blessing of Abraham — Abraham's blessing was to be counted as righteous by God. This same blessing was made possible to all men by what Jesus did on the cross.

might come upon the Gentiles — Thus the Gentiles have joined Father Abraham. They are accepted to share his blessing on the basis of faith, not on the basis of nationality or proselyte circumcision as the Jews had supposed.

that we might receive the promise of the Spirit through faith — This verse ties together the first three arguments of this chapter. (See comments on verse two for complete list.) The promised *Spirit* is given to *sons of Abraham* on the basis of *faith, not law.* This truth was crucial to correcting the problem of legalism in Galatia.

STUDY QUESTIONS:

1. Why did Paul call the Galatians "foolish" and even "bewitched"?
2. Had they seen the crucifixion of Jesus?
3. What is the argument of the first five verses?
4. How would they have known when it was that they received the Spirit?
5. Why don't we have the same miracles?
6. What did Abraham do in Gen. 15:6 that caused God to pronounce him righteous?
7. In what sense did the gospel exist even in the time of Abraham?
8. Why, specifically, does the law bring a curse over our heads?
9. In what way did the form of Jesus' execution connect him with the curse?
10. What does "redeem" mean?
11. How would you summarize the three arguments of this lesson?

Lesson Six
(3:15-29)

The Law and the Promise (3:15-20)

15 To give a human example, brethren: no one annuls even a man's will, or adds to it, once it has been ratified. 16 Now the promises were made to Abraham and to his offspring. It does not say, "And to offsprings," referring to many; but, referring to one, "And to your offspring," which is Christ. 17 This is what I mean: the law, which came four hundred and thirty years afterward, does not annul a covenant previously ratified by God, so as to make the promise void. 18 For if the inheritance is by the law, it is no longer by promise; but God gave it to Abraham by a promise.

19 Why then the law? It was added because of transgressions, till the offspring should come to whom the promise had been made; and it was ordained by angels through an intermediary. 20 Now an intermediary implies more than one; but God is one.

Paul is not ready to rest his case. There are still many more good reasons why faith is superior to law. Having proved this point with scripture, he now turns to example and illustration from everyday life. Even these, as you will see, are also supported by God's Word.

V. 15 **To give a human example, brethren** — The very first word in the Greek text of this verse is "brothers." Paul is not writing off the entire church as lost. To those who still were listening he makes his appeal. This fourth argument of chapter three is based on an experience of everyday life: a man's last will and testament.

no one annuls even a man's will — It was well known by Paul's readers that once a man's will goes into effect, it could not be changed. Specifically, once a man has written his will and then has died, and once the will is validated by the authorities, no one can come along and start changing its provisions. How much more, then, is the last will and testament (or covenant) of God unchangeable!

The word for a man's will in this verse is the same word used for the "covenant" of God in verse seventeen. It is an arrangement made by one party with full power, which the other party may accept or reject, but cannot alter. If two people were making an equal partnership agreement, a different word was used. The covenant between God and man is a grant, not a partnership. We can accept or reject the gift of salvation, but we cannot do enough to be worthy of it, nor can we change the terms of our acceptance.

or adds to it — In other words, once God established the covenant of salvation in Christ, no one has the right to add legalism to it.

once it has been ratified — Once a man has died and the authorities have approved his will as genuine, there are no more changes. Before ratification, of course, changes may be made. The point at which God's covenant was ratified will be discussed in verse seventeen.

V. 16 **Now the promises were made** — Just as there were two kinds of covenants in Greek (one-way grant and equal partnership), there are two kinds of promises. One kind of promise is obtained by negotiation, where each party gives and takes. The other kind of promise is a gift graciously bestowed, without receiving equal value in return. This is the word always used in the New Testament of the divine promise.

to Abraham and to his offspring — In Genesis 12:7 and thereafter, God made the promises to "Abraham and his seed." In the original Hebrew the form of the word is singular (although they would have thought of "seed" in a collective sense, just as we do in English: "to buy seed for planting.") Paul calls attention to the grammatical feature of "seed," not "seeds," and makes the application to the one special descendant Jesus Christ. The ultimate fulfillment of the promise did not lie in the Jewish people, as they had thought, but in Christ.

V. 17 **This is what I mean** — God made a promise to Abraham, and then ratified that promise or covenant. Four hundred and thirty years later the law came along. The law did not mean that God was cancelling his previous commitment, nor did it mean He was changing it in any way.

Some people find a problem in the dating of the 430 years. According to Exodus 12:40, the time between Abraham and Moses must have been

CHAPTER 3   GALATIANS 3:15-20

much more than 430 years, because the Israelites spent that much time in Egypt. And the stay in Egypt began long after the time of Abraham. There is a simple explanation. The word "ratify" means to make sure, or make firm. A man's will is not ratified when he first writes it, but when it first begins to take effect. The first part of God's promise to Abraham which took effect was that his descendants would stay four centuries in "a land not their own." (Gen. 15:13) The promise was thus "made sure" when Joseph and his brothers went to Egypt. From that point until the time of Moses was 430 years.

so as to make the promise void — It is wrong to think of God as abandoning his first plans and switching to another arrangement or dispensation. From the very beginning, in fact before the beginning (I Pet. 1:20), it has been God's plan to grant salvation through the sacrifice of Christ.

V. 18 **For if the inheritance is by the law** — The right to eternal life is either earned as a wage, or received as a gracious gift (Rom. 4:1-5). It cannot be both; it must be one or the other. Which is it?

God gave it to Abraham by a promise — Since this inheritance cannot be based on both law and promise, the Old Testament tells us which: the promise. Likewise, we can put our trust in God's ability to keep His promises, or our ability to keep His laws. One or the other — but not both!

V. 19 **Why then the law?** — At this point someone might well complain, "If what you say is true, there was never any need for the Law in the first place!" Was the Law of God a bad idea from the very beginning?

It was added because of transgressions — The law was added to show men how guilty they are of breaking God's standards of right and wrong. There was nothing wrong with the Law — there was something wrong with men. The Law was needed to show men how flawed and imperfect they were, and to show them how badly they need salvation.

till the offspring should come — God never intended the Law to be permanent. It was to prepare men for the coming of the offspring (Jesus), by pointing out how bad their sin was.

ordained by angels through an intermediary — God delivered the Law to Moses through angels (Acts 7:38, 53 and Heb. 2:2). The Greek version of the Old Testament also teaches this in Deut. 33:2. Just exactly how this was, we do not know. The point is this: Unlike the work of Christ (Heb. 1:1-4), God did not deal directly with His people when He gave the Law.

V. 20 **Intermediary implies more than one; but God is one** — When Christ dealt with men directly, as God in the flesh, it reflected more the true nature of God. He is not divided into levels or degrees. He is one. The covenant of grace was delivered directly; the covenant of law was second-hand.

Sons No Longer Under Law (3:21-29)

21 Is the law then against the promises of God? Certainly not; for if a law had been given which could make alive, then righteousness would indeed be by the law. 22 But the scripture consigned all things to sin, that what was promised to faith in Jesus Christ might be given to those who believe.

23 Now before faith came, we were confined under the law, kept under restraint until faith should be revealed. 24 So that the law was our custodian until Christ came, that we might be justified by faith. 25 But now that faith has come, we are no longer under a custodian; 26 for in Christ Jesus you are all sons of God, through faith. 27 For as many of you as were baptized into Christ have put on Christ. 28 There is neither Jew nor Greek, there is neither slave nor free, there is neither male nor female; for you are all one in Christ Jesus. 29 And if you are Christ's, then you are Abraham's offspring, heirs according to promise.

V. 21 Is the law then against the promises of God? — It might seem that the law and the promises are competing against each other, but they are not. They were each given by God to accomplish a specific purpose, and each succeeded in the task to which it was appointed. Since each was a necessary part of God's plan, there was no conflict.

if a law had been given which could make alive — It was never the purpose of the law to justify or make alive. The purpose of the law was to expose sin, and it did this very well. After the law did its job, then the promised grace in Christ Jesus stepped in to bring spiritual life. There is no conflict. It is only when people try to use the law to bring life — which it was never intended to do — that any problem exists.

V. 22 But the scripture consigned all things to sin — Before God could give life, men had to know the reality of their death. The law proved all men to be sinners, as later O.T. scriptures declare (Ps. 14:1-3; Is. 59:7-8; etc.).

that what was promised . . . might be given — The stern severity of the law was a necessary prelude to grace. God did not ever condemn men out of simple hatred or hostility. To the contrary, God's judgment has been shown to bring men to His grace. Once it had been shown that salvation could not be earned by anyone, God could then give it as a free gift to those who put their faith in Jesus Christ.

V. 23 Now before faith came — Here "faith" is the belief and trust in the revealed Son of God. Abraham had faith in the future fulfillment of a promise; we have faith in the Christ who has actually stepped into history. Until Christ came, the law was necessary — in a way that is explained in the following verses.

we were confined under the law — God's people in the Old Testament had to be confined or "held prisoner" for their own well-being. The law was used to "guard and keep watch over" them, as a literal translation of the Greek would show. This protective custody helped shield God's people from their own sinful urges, but it was not His best and final remedy.

kept under restraint — The best the law could ever do was to act as a restraint on people. It did not draw people closer to God; it merely fenced them in to keep them from drifting farther away. Law restrains, but love constrains. The first is a negative force, but the second is positive.

V. 24 **So that the law was our custodian** — In Greek and Roman society the custodian (*paidagogos*) was a household slave, purchased to help care for the children. He would guard them from danger, discipline them, and direct their physical exercise and body development. He was not a teacher; rather, he would escort the children to and from school. Some translations of this verse use the word "schoolmaster" or "tutor," but the custodian would have taught only the most rudimentary things. The real teaching was done by someone else.

Paul's readers would have immediately caught the application of this illustration. While the law had helped to guide, guard, and discipline God's children, its main purpose was to bring them to the point of real education — Christ.

until Christ came — The Greek says literally that the law was our custodian "unto Christ." This could mean the law helped to bring us to Christ (by convicting us of sin), or it could mean the law was in charge of us only until the arrival of Christ.

that we might be justified by faith — The law was never intended to be more than a temporary aid. From the very beginning the law was destined to be removed from any authority, just as soon as the real Authority came. Then man could be justified by trusting in the final Authority, rather than by submitting to the slave.

V. 25 **But now that faith has come** — As in verse twenty-three, "faith" is commitment to the revealed object of faith, namely, Jesus Christ. He is our true teacher (Eph. 4:20).

we are no longer under a custodian — God's law in the Old Testament has served its purpose; it has prepared the world for Christ. Now it is taken out of the way. The children have come of age. The custodian has been dismissed.

It is astonishing that people could read these verses in Galatians and still defend the law as binding on us. To force men to stay under the rule of the custodian is to doom them to immaturity. Babysitters and nannies may be fine for children, but no adult is under guardianship unless he is mentally or physically incompetent.

The law was our custodian, but when we commit ourselves in faith to Christ we are no longer under it.

V. 26 In Christ Jesus you are all sons of God — God's maturing children have outgrown their nanny. Jesus Christ has made this possible for us, as children of God. But in addition to our freedom from legalism, something more has been won for us by Christ. As free sons of God we also enjoy equality with one another. Because we came into the family of God on the same basis, we all share a common fellowship and unity. The first and most emphatic word in the Greek sentence is "all."

through faith — This verse joins together two important benefits for the Christian. First, we are freed from legalism; second, we are freed from divisive class status. Indeed, these two are intertwined. For if we were saved by our own merit, we would be appointed to certain levels and grades on the basis of who we were and what we had accomplished. Since we are saved through faith, neither legalism or status mean anything to us any longer.

V. 27 For as many of you as were baptized into Christ — The entrance into the new covenant relationship with God is the act of baptism. There is, of course, no merit or magic in the water. What counts is the humble surrender to God. All men approach the Creator in the same way — on their knees. God has designated that we submit to the richly symbolic act (Rom. 6;1-4), and we have no right to quibble. (Acts 2:38; 22:16)

All Greek dictionaries, incidentally, agree that the word *baptizo* means "immerse." (See John 3:23 and Acts 8:35-38).

have put on Christ — In Christian baptism we "clothe ourselves" with Christ. We will not stand before God in the filthy rags of our own attempted goodness, but in the white robes of Christ's righteousness. (See Isa. 64:6 and Rev. 6:11).

V. 28 There is neither Jew nor Greek — Since we "clothe ourselves" with Christ (see vs. 27) we all look alike! Jews and Greeks (representing all Gentiles) are no longer divided, for "the dividing wall of hostility" has been taken out of the way (Eph. 2:14). Probably no racial prejudice or national hatred ever surpassed the intensity of animosity between Jew and Gentile, but this animosity is ended in Christ.

there is neither slave nor free — Roman slavery was at its worst at the birth of Christ. Masters had the legal right to torture or kill slaves, since they were mere property. But now, in Christ Jesus, the free man and the slave stand before God on equal footing. Both are unworthy; both are accepted on the merit of God's Son.

there is neither male nor female — Ancient society, including the Jews, usually took a disparaging view of women. Since women could not receive circumcision, they were less than full participants in the old covenant. The Talmud (the official Jewish book of traditions and scripture commentary) has some very harsh statements in this regard: "May

CHAPTER 3   GALATIANS 3:21-29

the words of the Torah be burned, they should not be handed over to women." "Women are greedy, inquisitive, lazy, vain, and frivolous." "Happy is he whose children are males, and woe to him whose children are females." "Ten measures of empty-headedness have come upon the world, nine having been received by women, and one by the rest of the world." "Conversation should not be held with a woman, even if she is your wife."

Women are saved in Christ on the same terms as men. This does not, however, cancel out the separate and distinct roles of men and women in the home or in the church. It was after Paul wrote Galatians that he affirmed the woman's appointed role (I Co. 11:3-16; 14:33-36; I Tim. 2:8-15). The context in Galatians deals with eligibility for salvation.

The Jewish Book of Prayer, which dates back to at least 200 A.D., contains this prayer (possibly known to Paul as a young Pharisee):

> O Lord, Ruler of the Universe
> I thank thee that thou didst not
> make me a Gentile
>   or a Slave
>   or a Woman.

Even the order is the same as in this verse. But in Christ we are all saved on the same basis.

V. 29 And if you are Christ's — Verses 26 and 28 have just affirmed that we are Christ's. Because this is so, we share in the two wonderful consequences named in this verse.

then you are Abraham's offspring — It is not our bloodline, but our faith that makes us descendants of Abraham. The Jews who trusted in their ancestry have been replaced by Christians, who trust in their Saviour.

heirs according to promise — Our faith in Christ not only makes us descendants of Abraham, but also makes us heirs of his estate. What was coming to Abraham is now also coming to us; namely, justification by faith.

STUDY QUESTIONS:

1. How was God's promise to Abraham like a man's will?
2. What does Paul conclude from the fact that "offspring" was singular in God's promise to Abraham?
3. Was it 430 years from Abraham to Moses?
4. If the law could not save us, why did God give it?
5. Is law opposed to promises? Is it proper to say that one succeeded

and one failed? (See v. 21.)
6. What were the duties of the custodian? In what way did the law do similar things for God's children?
7. What happens when a person is baptized?
8. What categories became irrelevant in the salvation of mankind? What other categories might be named today?
9. Are women, then, the same as men in every respect, so far as God is concerned?
10. What two blessings are ours since we belong to Christ through faith?

Lesson Seven
(4:1-16)

No Longer Slaves (4:1-7)
1 I mean that the heir, as long as he is a child, is no better than a slave, though he is the owner of all the estate; 2 but he is under guardians and trustees until the date set by the father. 3 So with us; when we were children, we were slaves to the elemental spirits of the universe. 4 But when the time had fully come, God sent forth his Son, born of woman, born under the law, 5 to redeem those who were under the law, so that we might receive adoption as sons. 6 And because you are sons, God has sent the Spirit of his Son into our hearts, crying, "Abba! Father!" 7 So through God you are no longer a slave but a son, and if a son then an heir.

The true heirs of God's promises are those who are children of Abraham by faith. Before Christ came, these children were minors, under the guardianship of the law. As such, they were no better than slaves! But then, in the fulness of time, God sent Jesus to redeem us and God's children came of age. Why then, would the Galatians want to go back to their infancy and become under law again? Paul is now set to demonstrate just how foolish that would be.

V. 1 **I mean that the heir, as long as he is a child** — Paul did not want to imply that the Jews of earlier centuries were excluded from the promises and were not counted as heirs. So long as they had faith in God, they were included, but not as free adults. They were like minor children under a guardian.

is no better than a slave — Even the child in a king's castle is no better than a slave. While it may be true that he is legally entitled to inherit his father's riches and perhaps even a throne, right now he is governed by a nanny who even tells him when to blow his nose! Little children have no freedom because they are unable to handle it. This is no problem, as long as they show signs of eventual maturity. What a tragedy, though, when a mature adult reverts to this level! This would be the situation if they returned to legalism.

V. 2 **But he is under guardians and trustees** — This is simply to restate the situation of the custodian in the last chapter. The children of Israel were subject to the law as their guardian and trustee.

until the date set by the father — The minor child does not actually receive what is coming to him until the time specified by his father. A father's will might specify that his son should receive what has been held in trust when the son reaches the age of twenty-one. Likewise in dealing with the children of Israel, God picked a certain point in history at which his people would mature from infancy to adulthood. This point in history is named in verse four.

V. 3 **So with us; when we were children** — Before we came to Christ we were in the childhood of the human race and were under bondage. This bondage under law applied to both Jews and Gentiles, although in varying degree (see Rom. 2:14-15). It does not seem to matter whether the Galatian Christians had formerly been Jews or idol worshippers. If they now accepted legalism, they were reverting to childhood.

we were slaves to the elemental spirits of the universe — The word "spirits" is not in the Greek text and is entirely unwarranted here. Although this translation is found in the RSV and certain other recent versions, the earliest known use of the word "elemental" in this connection is the 4th century. It is a violent change of context to introduce the worship of "spirits" into the argument.

The right translation would be "slaves to the elementary things of the world." The "elementary things" is simply another way of saying "the law." This is confirmed by what immediately precedes (3:24 and 4:2), as well as by what immediately follows (4:5).

V. 4 **But when the time had fully come** — The Father appointed a time when His children should come of age. This appointed time in history was the 1st century, when the stage was set and the world was ripe for the introduction of Christianity. Roman law had brought world peace and Roman roads made travel easier than at any other century before or since, until quite recently. Consider what this meant to evangelism. The Greeks contributed a common language known in all nations

CHAPTER 4   GALATIANS 4:1-7

and a religious climate that was desperate for a better answer. Both the religion and the philosophy failed to bring man the solution for his problems. The Jews contributed the synagogue and the Septuagint. The synagogue had become the replacement for the Temple in nearly every ancient city, and was a gospel beachhead in every city where Paul preached. The Septuagint, the Greek translation of the Old Testament, was carried by Jews into all countries, and spread the prophecies of a coming Messiah. There seems to have been a universal expectation and need of a Saviour.

God sent forth his Son — One might have expected the Son to make a spectacular entrance onto such a carefully prepared stage. No luxury would be too great; no fanfare would be too glorious for the Incarnate God.

born of woman — He who was fully God became also fully man. He entered the human race as a helpless baby born to an inexperienced young mother. The virgin wrapped the Son of God in strips of cloth and laid him in a feed trough.

born under the law — In order for Jesus to be able to offer himself to pay the penalty of our sin, he had to be subject to law as a man and live up to its requirements. He met the demands of the law with his life, and satisfied our penalty under law with his death.

V. 5 **to redeem those who were under the law** — Christ "bought us back" from the curse of the law (see comments on 3:13). It was necessary to become man, to save man. In the midst of this discussion about people being "slaves" under law, it is all the more appropriate to speak of Jesus "buying them back."

so that we might receive adoption as sons — Now the illustration of our relationship to God changes from that of a baby growing up to that of a person being adopted. Adoption was fairly common in the ancient world. Among other things, the adoption brought about the following benefits: (1) a new name, (2) an inheritance, and (3) a cancellation of previous debts and obligations.

V. 6 **And because you are sons** — We are not working our way into God's good graces. He likes us and loves us because we are his children.

God has sent the Spirit of his Son into our hearts — God first sent his Son into the world (4:4), then his Spirit into our hearts. The Holy Spirit is the Spirit of Christ, as well as the Spirit of God. (See John 14:15-24, especially verse 23.) God has set the Holy Spirit on each of his children as a seal (Eph. 1:13-14), and any one who does not have the Spirit of Christ dwelling in him is simply not a part of the family (Rom. 8:9).

crying, "Abba! Father!" — "Abba" was the Aramaic word for "father" used in the intimacy of the family. The term expresses a feeling of love, confidence, and intimate fellowship. It does not, however, imply any flippancy or lack of respect as do sometimes the words "Pop" or "Daddy." (Rom. 8:15).

V. 7 **So through God** — Not through yourselves, but only through God's work is this blessing possible. All your efforts to work your way into salvation are futile.

you are no longer a slave but a son — This is the grand conclusion. We are not babies or slaves who need to be constantly guarded. We are grown sons, who have inherited the blessing of the Father.

How Can You Turn Back? (4:8-16)

8 Formerly, when you did not know God, you were in bondage to beings that by nature are no gods; 9 but now that you have come to know God, or rather to be known by God, how can you turn back again to the weak and beggarly elemental spirits, whose slaves you want to be once more? 10 You observe days, and months, and seasons, and years! 11 I am afraid I have labored over you in vain.

12 Brethren, I beseech you, become as I am, for I also have become as you are. You did me no wrong; 13 you know it was because of a bodily ailment that I preached the gospel to you at first; 14 and though my condition was a trial to you, you did not scorn or despise me, but received me as an angel of God, as Christ Jesus. 15 What has become of the satisfaction you felt? For I bear you witness that, if possible, you would have plucked out your eyes and given them to me. 16 Have I then become your enemy by telling you the truth?

V. 8 **Formerly, when you did not know God** — Most of the Christians in Galatia came from a pagan background, rather than Jewish. Their knowledge of the divine was limited to idols and Greek mythology.

you were in bondage to beings that by nature are no gods — Whether they had been Gentiles serving lifeless idols or Jews serving the law, the bondage was the same. For the Gentile Christian to go back into the Jewish law was just as bad as reverting to paganism. This is the rather surprising teaching of verses 8 and 9.

V. 9 **to know God, or rather to be known by God** — They had come out of idolatry into truth. But even more important than what a man comes to know is what God knows about that man. This puts the emphasis on the part of God in bringing about salvation, rather than on the part of man.

how can you turn back again to the weak and beggarly elemental spirits — As discussed in verse three of this chapter, the weak and beggarly "elemental things" are the law. Pagans who have now become Christians must not revert to law-keeping and attempting to appease an ill-tempered god. In the area of making men righteous the law is bankrupt; it has nothing to offer.

V. 10 **You observe days, months, seasons, and years!** — The Jews observed Sabbath days, first of the month sacrifices, annual seasons of feasting (Passover, Tabernacles, Atonement, etc.), and special years, such as the year of Jubilee. The Galatians were observing these "holy days" as well, thinking to gain favor with God.

V. 11 **I am afraid I have labored over you in vain** — If the Galatians now turned to legalism, all Paul's efforts and all the persecution he endured would be for nothing. Not for this had he delivered them from slavery to freedom!

V. 12 **Brethren, I beseech you** — Paul has appealed to authority, he has appealed to argument, and now his appeal is this simple plea: I beg you!

become as I am, for I also have become as you are — "I am free from the law (just like a Gentile), and you Christian Gentiles are free from the law, too." Paul had gone from servitude to freedom; they were going from freedom to servitude.

V. 13 **Because of a bodily ailment that I preached** — When Paul first came to Galatia he suffered from some physical ailment. Had it not been for this affliction, he apparently would have gone on to some other destination. While he paused to recuperate, then, he preached the gospel to them.

What was the problem? Some suggest Paul got malaria in the lowlands of Pamphylia and went to the higher altitudes of Galatia for relief. Others see epilepsy as the problem, noting the use of "despise" in the next verse. Others find the affliction to be eye trouble (see vs. 15), which was common in the Roman world. Migraine headaches, broken bones from the stoning, and many other ideas may be found. Whatever the ailment, Paul first prayed for deliverance (II Cor. 12:7-10) and then learned to let God's strength replace his own weakness.

V. 14 **Though my condition was a trial to you** — Whatever the nature of the affliction, it must have been visible and repulsive. It provided a real "temptation" to the Galatians to reject Paul and turn away.

you did not scorn or despise me — The word "scorn" meant to regard as worthless and treat with contempt. To "despise" meant literally "to spit out at." Whenever sick people — especially people with epilepsy — came too close to someone, that person would spit in the direction of the sick man. This was supposed to protect the person from the spirits of sickness. Paul's ailment, whatever it was, could well have caused the Galatians to scorn and despise him. To their credit, they did not.

but received me as an angel of God — They listened to him as God's own messenger. Why won't they listen to him now?

THIRTEEN LESSONS ON GALATIANS

V. 15 **What has become of the satisfaction you felt?** — Their "satisfaction" was a sense of happiness and blessedness. The same word is used for "blessed" in each of the beatitudes. When Paul preached Christ to them, they knew they were getting something good — something from God.

you would have plucked out your eyes — They would have done anything for Paul. The specific mention of "eyes" perhaps points to eye trouble as Paul's ailment. This may be connected with the Damascus blinding and healing when "scales fell" (Acts 9:18), his failure to recognize the High Priest (Acts 23:2-5), his use of a secretary in writing (Rom. 16:22), and the large letters written by his own hand at the end of this same epistle (6:11). These may or may not add up to eye trouble.

V. 16 **Have I then become your enemy by telling you the truth?** — How terribly wrong that the people who had received Paul so graciously and who would have done anything for him should now count him as their enemy because he told them the truth! Surely this would clear the air and bring them to their senses!

STUDY QUESTIONS:

1. How is a little child no better than a slave?
2. How is the child/slave situation similar to being under the law?
3. What historical indications do we have that "the time had fully come"?
4. What did adoption accomplish under Roman law, and what does it accomplish for us?
5. What is the meaning of "Abba! Father!"?
6. In what way was serving lifeless idol gods equivalent to turning back to Jewish legalism? (See vs. 8 & 9.)
7. Should the Christian observe "holy" days? If we keep Sunday as the Lord's Day, what should be our attitude and motivation?
8. How was Paul's condition a trial to them?
9. Why mention plucking out the eyes?
10. What was the point of going back and reviewing how it was when Paul first went to Galatia?

Lesson Eight

(4:17-31)

True and False Concern (4:17-20)

17 They make much of you, but for no good purpose; they want to shut you out, that you may make much of them. 18 For a good purpose it is always good to be made much of, and not only when I am present with you. 19 My little children, with whom I am again in travail until Christ be formed in you! 20 I could wish to be present with you now and to change my tone, for I am perplexed about you.

Paul has taken a break in his series of logical arguments to make an impassioned personal appeal. They are his children, they are in danger, and he cares! Finally the chapter will close with one last grand argument: the allegory of Abraham's two sons.

V. 17 **They make much of you** — False teachers, then and now, will literally "bubble over" in their enthusiasm for their converts. They will smother a person with attention and concern, until that person is convinced that no one in the world cares about them like this new teacher of new truth. Especially is this the case when the convert is well-known and prominent. Indians collect scalps, and cowboys notch their guns, but none is so proud as a proselyter with a new conquest.

but for no good purpose — It is selfish pride, rather than sincere concern, that motivates the false teacher to make converts. What is your

THIRTEEN LESSONS ON GALATIANS

motivation for making converts? Are you even motivated at all?

they want to shut you out — The Judaizers wanted to shut out the Galatian Christians from God's grace and from fellowship with God's whole family. They wanted to draw a tight little circle of believers in their own sect. We must take warning from this that we do not accept any dividing lines except those drawn by God Himself.

that you may make much of them — The real reason for the missionary zeal of the false teacher is his own selfish pride. The concern is false.

V. 18 **For a good purpose it is always good to be made much of** — People like to be appreciated and loved. It is only natural and right that we should want people to care about us. It is in this good sense that we should "outdo one another in showing honor." However, all this attention can be perverted. When one comes to expect or demand attention because he is a big shot, or when one craves attention because he feels so inferior, it is no longer a healthy thing.

not only when I am present with you — The sharpness of this rebuke is thinly veiled. The Galatians had been guilty of double-dealing duplicity. In Paul's presence they had honored him and respected his authority. Behind his back they rejected him and turned to other teachers.

V. 19 **My little children** — It was appropriate in two ways that Paul should address the Galatian Christians as "my little children." First, they were won to Christ by Paul's preaching and were thus his children in the faith. Second, they were acting in a very immature fashion, being "carried about by every wind of doctrine" (Eph. 4:14).

with whom I am again in travail — The word "travail" is a translation of the specific Greek word for labor pains at the birth of a baby. With great spiritual and physical anguish Paul had brought these people to the new birth into Christ. In a sense, however, their birth was incomplete. Now Paul is again in that same anguish to bring their conversion to completion. This would be accomplished when they let go of legalism and efforts to save themselves, and yielded completely to Christ, to let Him live His life through them.

until Christ be formed in you! — The only ultimate deliverance from the bondage of the law is to be re-created in the image of our Creator (Eph. 4:24; Col. 3:10). So long as we operate on the level of sinful self we will need constant restraint to keep us out of trouble. It is only when we die to self and are reborn in the nature of Christ that we can experience real freedom. This conversion process does not occur instantly, but over a lifetime. The problem in Galatia was that the process had ceased to occur at all.

V. 20 **I could wish to be present with you now** — Paul here expresses regret that he must deal with their problem by epistle, rather than by a personal visit. We do not know exactly what circumstances prevented

CHAPTER 4   GALATIANS 4:21-31

such a visit.
   to change my tone — Much of the preceding letter has been stern, even harsh. Paul fears that the sharpness of his pen has not adequately conveyed the emotion of his heart. If only the Galatians could look into his face, his eyes, and know what he felt toward them!
   for I am perplexed about you — Paul was at his wit's end. The Greek word originally meant "not having a way to cross a river." Just as a man who looks helplessly across the river he cannot ford, Paul felt a sense of despair. He was so far away, and they were so misled, that the situation at this moment looked grim.

The Allegory of Two Sons (4:21-31)
21 Tell me, you who desire to be under law, do you not hear the law? 22 For it is written that Abraham had two sons, one by a slave and one by a free woman. 23 But the son of the slave was born according to the flesh, the son of the free woman through promise. 24 Now this is an allegory: these women are two covenants. One is from Mount Sinai, bearing children for slavery; she is Hagar. 25 Now Hagar is Mount Sinai in Arabia; she corresponds to the present Jerusalem, for she is in slavery with her children. 26 But the Jerusalem above is free, and she is our mother. 27 For it is written,
   "Rejoice, O barren one that dost not bear;
   break forth and shout, thou who art not in travail;
   for the desolate hath more children
   than she who hath a husband."
28 Now we, brethren, like Isaac, are children of promise. 29 But as at that time he who was born according to the flesh persecuted him who was born according to the Spirit, so it is now. 30 But what does the scripture say? "Cast out the slave and her son; for the son of the slave shall not inherit with the son of the free woman. 31 So, brethren, we are not children of the slave but of the free woman.

   V. 21   **Tell me, you who desire to be under law** — Paul has one last grand argument for the would-be legalists. He invites those who are so enthusiastic for law (any law) to listen to a beautifully drawn allegory from law (the law — the one revealed by God to Moses).
   The allegory is an extended parable or metaphor. It says, "This is like that in the following points . . ." It lists point by point the similarities between two things, drawing a conclusion or moral at the end. This form of argument was popular in the ancient world, and would probably have had great persuasive power among the Galatians. (If the point you are making is true, some form of illustration may help people see the

reasonableness of your assertion. However, a good illustration does not prove anything. The point must first be proved true, then illustrated. This is what Paul has done in chapters three and four.)

V. 22 **For it is written that Abraham had two sons** — You will want to read Genesis 16:1-16 and 21:1-10 to review this part of Abraham's life. Several points in each passage will be selected for comparison.

one by a slave — The son of Hagar, Sarah's handmaid, was named Ishmael.

one by a free woman — The son of Sarah, Abraham's wife, was named Isaac. Isaac's name appears in verse 28, but Ishmael's name is not used.

V. 23 **born according to the flesh** — When Abraham and Sarah saw no indication of a fulfillment to the promise of offspring, they decided to take matters into their own hands. Sarah gave her handmaid to Abraham to conceive children in her place. (See Genesis 16.) It was precisely this action which made the birth of Ishmael like the attempts of the Judaizers to justify themselves. Lacking faith in God, they try to do it their own way.

the son of the free woman through promise — The birth of Isaac stood in sharp contrast to the birth of Ishmael. Read carefully Gen. 21:1 and notice where the emphasis is placed. "THE LORD visited Sarah AS HE SAID, and THE LORD did to Sarah AS HE HAD PROMISED. And Sarah conceived...." (Emphasis mine.) This wording in Genesis even led some Jewish theologians to construe this as a "fatherless birth!" The essential point, though, is clear. Ishmael was born as a result of human effort; Isaac was born as a result of the promise of God. Thirteen years after the birth of Ismael, God blessed Abraham and Sarah, and Isaac was conceived.

The application of the whole allegory is dependent upon this verse. When Abraham tried to do it for himself, the result was ultimately cast out. When Abraham trusted God's promise and waited for God's blessing, the heir was born. Such is the picture of works versus faith.

V. 24 **Now this is an allegory** — In contrast to many ancient allegories, this one is quite simple and direct. The main points of contrast may be seen in the following chart:

TWO SONS

ISHMAEL	ISAAC
Born according to flesh	Born through promise
Mother — Hagar	Mother — Sarah
Slave	Free
Mt. Sinai	(Mt. Zion)
Present Jerusalem	Jerusalem above
Is in slavery	Is free
Born for slavery	Born for freedom
Persecutor	Persecuted
Born according to flesh	Born according to Spirit
Cast out	Made heir

CHAPTER 4   GALATIANS 4:21-31

these women are two covenants — Long before the time of either Moses or Jesus, the two covenants were pre-figured in the lives of Hagar and Sarah. When the Galatian people choose which covenant they will come under, they should notice the ultimate outcome assigned to their choice. Legalists cast their lot with Ishmael; true Christians trust God for forgiveness and cast their lot with Isaac.

One is from Mount Sinai — God gave the Law to Moses at Mt. Sinai in the midst of thunder, lightning, and smoke. At the blast of a trumpet the mountain quaked and the people trembled. (See Exodus 19:16-21 and Hebrews 12:18-24.) The obvious contrast, Mt. Zion, is not mentioned.

bearing children for slavery — Just as Hagar's son became a slave, so all children of the law are doomed to slavery and fear. Notice how well this illustrates the principles of Gal. 3:10 — 4:9.

V. 25 **Now Hagar is Mount Sinai in Arabia** — Although there are certain traditions that *Hagar* was another name for Sinai, or the name of a nearby city, or a word meaning "rock," I think it best to understand simply that Paul arbitrarily connected Hagar and Sinai. He was justified in making this connection by the clear application shown in verse twenty-three.

she corresponds to the present Jerusalem — Paul draws a line from Sinai to Jerusalem, connecting the origin of the law with the present headquarters of the legalists.

she is in slavery with her children — The temple in Jerusalem, with its sacrifices and rituals, represented the essence of the law. (The fact that Jerusalem was destroyed and the temple was torn down in 70 A.D., less than twenty years after the writing of this epistle, only serves to underscore the inferiority of the covenant law.) Legalists do not have much to look forward to.

V. 26 **But the Jerusalem above is free** — Christians are citizens of the heavenly kingdom (Phil. 3:20). Through the church we already participate in it (Heb. 12:22-24), while we also await the final consummation pictured in Rev. 21:2. We belong to this kingdom, and she is our mother, by virtue of our faith in the promises of God.

V. 27 **For it is written** — The quotation is from Isaiah 54:1. In that context it refers to the restoration of Judah following her captivity in Babylon. She is pictured as a forsaken or widowed wife, who is now wed to her Creator. The same sentiments fit very well in the case of Sarah, after she had been held in contempt by Hagar.

the desolate hath more children — She who could produce no children by her own ability has been blessed by God in such a way that now she out-produces her competitor. So we, who could not achieve our own righteousness, are blessed by God to have greater righteousness than legalistic law-keepers (Matt. 5:20).

V. 28 Now we, brethren, like Isaac — All those who take their stand on the promise of God's grace are truly "brethren" to Paul. They, like Isaac, are children of promise.

V. 29 But as at that time — When Isaac was weaned Abraham held a great feast in his honor (Gen. 21:8-10). Ishmael, Isaac's half-brother, was around fifteen years of age and was mocking the whole thing. At the request of Sarah, and with the approval of God, Abraham cast out this son with his slave mother.

The feeling of hostility persisted between the descendants of Ishmael and those of Isaac. In much the same way, Abraham's descendants according to the flesh (the Jews) were persecuting his descendants according to the Spirit (the Christians).

V. 30 But what does the scripture say? — Paul has shown many points of comparisons between Genesis and Galatia. (Review the chart with verse 24.) Now he is ready for the conclusion of the matter — the conclusion stated in the scripture itself.

Cast out the slave and her son — This course of action was suggested by Sarah (Gen. 21:10) and confirmed by God (Gen. 21:12). The son of the slave was disinherited and the child of promise inherited all things. Paul affirms that this same verdict will apply to those in slavery under the law and those who trust God's promise.

V. 31 So, brethren — This is the third time in this chapter that Paul has referred to his Galatian readers as "brethren." It is especially true in the light of our common ancestry through faith in Abraham's God that we are brothers and sisters in the same family.

not children of the slave but of the free — The Jews had always placed great stock in being the offspring of Abraham (Cf. Matt. 3:9). Their reliance upon this physical ancestry was now, ironically, the very thing that made them not his heirs. Legalists, whatever their family tree, are descended in attitude and spirit from Hagar the slave.

STUDY QUESTIONS:

1. Why are false teachers sometimes so very zealous? (See verse 17.)
2. Is the process of new birth completed at the point of conversion and baptism? (Verse 19)
3. How can Paul call the Galatians both his "children" (v. 19) and his "brethren" (v. 28 and 31)?
4. What is the background of the word "perplexed"?
5. Why might the allegory of Isaac and Ishmael be persuasive to the Galatians?
6. What is the key contrast regarding the birth of these two sons?

CHAPTER 4   GALATIANS 4:21-31

7. How do we earn the right to be citizens of the "Jerusalem above"?
8. Read 4:27 again and consider this question: Why does God always seem to favor the underdog?
9. Whose child are you? Are you trusting in yourself or in God?

Lesson Nine

(5:1-15)

Set Free To Be Free (5:1-6)

1 For freedom Christ has set us free; stand fast therefore, and do not submit again to a yoke of slavery.

2 Now I, Paul, say to you that if you receive circumcision, Christ will be of no advantage to you. 3 I testify again to every man who receives circumcision that he is bound to keep the whole law. 4 You are severed from Christ, you who would be justified by the law; you have fallen away from grace. 5 For through the Spirit, by faith, we wait for the hope of righteousness. 6 For in Christ Jesus neither circumcision nor uncircumcision is of any avail, but faith working through love.

The evidence has been offered; the arguments have been made. Now Paul is ready for his great conclusion: We are free because Christ has set us free! As free men we owe nothing to the bondage of legalism. And if we should ever go back and yield to this yoke of bondage, we would cease to be free, and we would cease to be in Christ.

V. 1 **For freedom Christ has set us free** — This is the good news of Galatians. This is the conclusion to which all the arguments of chapters 3 and 4 were leading. Christ set us free to live the life of freedom.

stand fast therefore — The Galatian Christians were facing both persecution and perverted teaching. As liberated slaves they must

CHAPTER 5   GALATIANS 5:1-6

cherish and defend their freedom. (A more complete translation of the Greek verb would be "take your stand and keep on standing.")

do not submit again to a yoke of slavery — This is a highly derogatory way to refer to keeping the law of Moses. Hebrews 6:4-6 pronounces a terrible verdict on those who forsake freedom in Christ and return to law-keeping. In a similar vein, II Pet. 2:21 says it would have been better for them never to have known the way of righteousness than after knowing it to turn back.

V. 2   **Now I, Paul, say to you** — On the basis of his apostolic authority, proved in chapters 1 and 2, Paul speaks the final word on this subject.

if you receive circumcision — The reference is not to past action, but to the future. "Now that you have the whole picture, what are you going to do? If you go ahead and chose circumcision anyway, Christ can do you no good."

Christ will be of no advantage to you — Christ cannot profit the legalist anything. The reason is that the legalist lacks faith — which is necessary to salvation. Concluding that Christ's sacrifice was not sufficient, he desperately tries to save himself. He is like the drowning man who tries to "help" the lifeguard save him by struggling to climb up out of the water. We can be saved only when we surrender. If Jesus is to save us, we must yield to His authority and trust Him. We must quit fighting to save ourselves and do whatever He tells us.

V. 3   **I testify again** — There is an air of solemn finality about what Paul says. Compare this repetition of vital truth (verses 2 and 3) with chapter one, verses 8 and 9.

To every man who receives circumcision — This has no application to modern circumcision practiced for reasons of hygiene. It applies to the man who chooses to wear the badge of law-keeping because he doubts the sufficiency of what Jesus did at Calvary.

that he is bound to keep the whole law — Circumcision was not merely an isolated commandment in the Old Testament. It signified entrance into the covenant relationship. It was the physical symbol of the whole law. If any man expects to earn God's favor through the law, he had better plan to be very busy, for there is an enormous task awaiting him.

V. 4   **You are severed from Christ** — Those who pledge allegiance to the law, through circumcision, cut themselves off from Christ. The word "severed" means having nothing more to do with, or being abolished from. It is the same word used in Rom. 7:2, where a married woman is "discharged from" the law binding her to her husband when the husband dies. Legalists are thus discharged from Christ and his atoning sacrifice when they try to depend upon the law.

you who would be justified by the law — This could also be translated "you who are trying to justify yourselves by law." One can trust in Jesus or in law, but not both.

you have fallen away from grace — To rely upon works is to reject grace. This verse teaches us two most important facts: (1) It is indeed possible to fall from grace and sever yourself from Christ. (2) In this context, at least, the way to fall from grace is to fall back on to works of law, rather than trusting God's promise.

The word for "fall away" was used of ships that had gone off course and were no longer heading for the intended destination. The word in this verse is not so strong as the word used in Heb. 6:6. That word was used of ships that were not only off course, but completely lost. Here in Galatians the possibility of return is in mind.

V. 5 **For through the Spirit, by faith** — We who sadly admit our inability to save ourselves can only cast ourselves upon God's mercy and grace. We look ahead to Judgment Day, where we will take our stand not upon works of law, but upon faith, through God's own Spirit.

we wait for the hope of righteousness — The verdict of innocence is eagerly awaited by those who trust in Jesus. We will not get what we deserve, but what He deserved! Just as our father Abraham, we do not stand in line to be paid for our services, but humbly await the gift of God's grace. (See Rom. 4:1-5)

V. 6 **For in Christ Jesus** — We have been baptized into Christ (Gal. 3:27) where the old divisions between male and female, free and slave, Jew and Greek are erased. God does not care whether a man has been circumcised or not. What does matter is whether that man is in Christ.

neither circumcision nor uncircumcision is of any avail — Paul is taking neither a pro-circumcision nor an anti-circumcision stand. It is neither the keeping nor the breaking of the old law that matters, since the law itself has been cancelled.

but faith working through love — What counts with God is faith — active, working faith. This phrase strikes the perfect balance between the two extremes of "faith only" vs. "working my way to Heaven." Faith which is inactive and unproductive is dead and worthless (James 2:14-26). Likewise, all efforts toward earning our own righteousness through good works are doomed to failure.

Does God expect good works or not? Are good works a necessary part of salvation, or are they not? Perhaps it can be explained in this way: God does not want works of law; He wants works of love. God does not want works produced by fear, attempting to earn salvation; He wants works produced by faith, responding in love because salvation has already been given.

A Little Bad Leaven (5:7-15)

7 You were running well; who hindered you from obeying the truth? 8 This persuasion is not from him who called you. 9 A little leaven leavens the whole lump. 10 I have confidence in the Lord that you will take no other view than mine; and he who is troubling you will bear his judgment, whoever he is. 11 But if I, brethren, still preach circumcision, why am I still persecuted? In that case the stumbling block of the cross has been removed. 12 I wish those who unsettle you would mutilate themselves!

13 For you were called to freedom, brethren, only do not use your freedom as an opportunity for the flesh, but through love be servants of one another. 14 For the whole law is fulfilled in one word, "you shall love your neighbor as your self." 15 But if you bite and devour one another take heed that you are not consumed by one another.

V. 7 **You were running well** — The Christian life is often described as a race (Heb. 12:1; II Tim. 4:7). In this race the Galatians got off to a good start by the preaching of Paul.

who hindered you from obeying the truth? — The word "hindered" alludes to the ancient military practice of cutting trenches across the road to stop an advancing army. The false teachers had put this kind of spiritual impediment in the way of the Galatians, when they persuaded them to turn from the true gospel.

V. 8 **This persuasion is not from him who called you** — This reminds us of the words of Paul in 1:6, "I am astonished that you are so quickly deserting him who called you."

V. 9 **A little leaven leavens the whole lump** — Just as one rotten apple can spoil the whole barrel, a little false teaching goes a long ways. The use of leaven to illustrate an evil influence was also used by Jesus in Matt. 16:6.

V. 10 **I have confidence** — Paul expresses confidence that his "brethren," as he calls them twice in the next three verses, will accept his epistle as truth. They will agree that the legalistic influence of the Judaizers is not from God. For similar expressions of confidence following stern rebukes, see Heb. 6:9 and 10:32-39.

he who is troubling you will bear his judgment — The false teacher should have a two-fold judgment. First, he should be exposed and rejected by the united church. Second, he will ultimately stand before God on Judgment Day.

V. 11 **But if I, brethren, still preach circumcision** — Apparently the false teacher(s) had even claimed that Paul still supported circumcision! (They could have pointed to Timothy, whom Paul had circumcised as an expedient for Jewish evangelism, Acts 16:3.) One verse is all that is needed to show the folly of such a claim.

the stumbling block of the cross — The cross of Christ was a major stumbling block to the Jews (I Cor. 1:23), who expected the Messiah to be a hero-king. They could not accept the shame-filled cross as the replacement for their own works of virtue. If the Jews could cling to circumcision and works when they became Christians, the stumbling block of the cross would be removed.

V. 12 **those who unsettle you** — The same word here for "unsettle" is used in Acts 21:38 of the man who "stirred up a revolt" and got a lot of people killed.

would mutilate themselves! — Those who make so much of circumcision ("cutting around") should go all the way and emasculate ("cutting off") themselves! Paul should not be thought crude or vengeful for this statement, for he was simply recommending that they follow their own teaching to its logical conclusion.

The Galatian readers would undoubtedly have thought of the pagan cult of Attis in nearby Phrygia. When priests of this religion were being initiated into their priesthood, they used wine and dance to work themselves into a frenzy and then castrated themselves. If the Galatians knew the O.T. Law, they would also remember that the eunuch was ineligible for the priesthood of the true God.

V. 13 **For you were called to freedom, brethren** — This echoes the triumphant cry of 5:1. God's plan and purpose for His people is that they should be free!

only do not use your freedom as an opportunity for the flesh — While verse one urged the Galatians not to lose their freedom, this verse urges them not to abuse it. Freedom from law is not intended to be lawlessness. Freedom must not be used as an opportunity ("point from which ships are launched") for the flesh. Rather, our freedom is to be a launching-pad for flight into higher and higher spiritual realms.

There are two ways in which the Christian can lose his freedom. One is by submitting to the false doctrine of legalism. The other is by yielding to his own selfish sinful nature (Rom. 6:12-22). To lose our freedom in either way results in slavery.

through love be servants of one another — We are set free not to do evil, but to do good — especially to one another. It is this application of our freedom which will be especially in view in chapter six. The force that motivates us to volunteer for slavery to each other is simply love.

V. 14 **For the whole law is fulfilled in one word** — As Paul explained in Romans 13:8-10, the man who truly loves his neighbor does not need any commandment to forbid him to steal or kill. Love tells him that, and much more. No legal code could ever be detailed enough to cover

CHAPTER 5   GALATIANS 5:7-15

all the territory encompassed in the one word — love.

"you shall love your neighbor as yourself" — Jesus quoted this law from Lev. 19:18 as being second only to the command to love God (Matt. 22:36-40). All that men have to do with one another is governed by this grand command: Love your neighbor as yourself.

But who is my neighbor? Who is included in the group I must love? The ancient Qumran sect, as known from the Dead Sea Scrolls, demanded strict observance of this scripture. But since "neighbor" included only the other members at Qumran, they were free to hate everyone else. Jesus taught that love must extend to include even our enemies (Matt. 5:43-48) and used a lowly Samaritan to illustrate real love (Luke 10:29-37). It is in this way that love carries us far beyond where law ever could.

V. 15 **But if you bite and devour one another** — If we reject love for one another as the highest good, we necessarily revert to the law of the jungle. It is every man for himself! The unity of the Galatian churches had no doubt been ruined by false doctrine, creating the enmity and strife mentioned in the next few verses.

take heed that you are not consumed by one another — If it is to be the law of the jungle, then they had better be on constant guard! The members of the Body will hack away at each other, until there is literally nothing left.

STUDY QUESTIONS:

1. Once we have been set free by Christ, how can we lose our freedom?
2. If a man receives circumcision, why is it necessary for him to keep the whole law?
3. Is it possible to "fall away" from grace? How?
4. How does our text resolve the Faith vs. Works controversy?
5. What is the picture behind the word "hindered" in verse seven?
6. Why is even a little false teaching so dangerous?
7. Why did those who believed in circumcision find the cross of Christ to be such a stumbling block?
8. Verse thirteen suggests both the wrong and the right use of Christian freedom. What are they?
9. How does love fulfill the law?
10. Who is your neighbor?

Lesson Ten

(5:16-21)

Works of the Flesh

16 But I say, walk by the Spirit, and do not gratify the desires of the flesh. 17 For the desires of the flesh are against the Spirit, and the desires of the Spirit are against the flesh; for these are opposed to each other, to prevent you from doing what you would. 18 But if you are led by the Spirit you are not under the law. 19 Now the works of the flesh are plain: immorality, impurity, licentiousness, 20 idolatry, sorcery, enmity, strife, jealousy, anger, selfishness, dissension, party spirit, 21 envy, drunkenness, carousing, and the like. I warn you, as I warned you before, that those who do such things shall not inherit the kingdom of God.

Christ did not set us free from bondage to the law only to have us yield to bondage to the flesh. To live as slaves to our own fleshly nature is directly contrary to the will of the Spirit for our lives. The Spirit and the flesh are at war within us. This lesson will set the stage for that battle and will catalogue the evil forces of the flesh. The next lesson will present the forces for good: the fruit of the Spirit.

V. 16   **But I say, walk by the Spirit** — In contrast to the self-seeking indulgence warned against in the preceding verses, the Christian must walk by the Spirit. The use of the word "walk" shows that the Christian life must be active and must be making progress. The fact that we are

CHAPTER 5 — GALATIANS 5:16-21

not under law but under grace does not exempt us from this walk. We who have life through the Spirit must walk by the Spirit.

do not gratify the desires of the flesh — The way in which Paul expressed this is very strong in the Greek. An expanded translation would read, "By no means shall you gratify...." When Paul wrote "the desires of the flesh" he was referring to the unredeemed nature of man at its worst.

V. 17 **For the desires of the flesh** — The appetites of the physical body are neither good nor bad; they are neutral. When they are satisfied within the framework of God's plan for mankind, they are good. When they are allowed to dominate a man's life with no restraining guidance from the Spirit, they are bad. If a man is hungry and his eyes see food, his flesh says, "Eat!" Under the appropriate circumstances, this appetite is very beneficial to the man. But if the food he sees belongs to someone else, it would be wrong to eat it. Regardless of this, the flesh says, "Eat!" Now the man's spirit must over rule his flesh, or fall into sin. The life in which flesh is allowed to run rampant will have total disregard for right and wrong. It is in this perspective of ultimate lawlessness that Paul is using the word "flesh."

the desires of the Spirit — While the ultimate goal of flesh is self-preservation and self-satisfaction, the aim of the Holy Spirit is for us to get in line with God's will. Our human spirits must surrender completely to the Holy Spirit, so that He becomes the governor of our lives. The man whose final authority is his flesh is no better than a brute animal. The man whose final authority is the Spirit is a child of God.

to prevent you from doing what you would — The conflict works both ways. The flesh interferes with the will of the Spirit, and the Spirit interferes with the will of the flesh. We necessarily surrender to one, and overcome the other.

V. 18 **But if you are led by the Spirit** — As the Christian walks through life (see vs. 16) he must follow the leading of the Spirit. But how is he to know which way the Spirit is leading? If he finds the will of the Spirit in the scriptures inspired by the Spirit, he is on solid ground. If he thinks to find the will of the Spirit in his own inner impulses and feelings, he is dangerously close to following the will of the flesh. Apart from the truth of God's Word, how can he tell whether his feelings are being generated by flesh or Spirit?

you are not under the law — While we are being led by the Spirit we are not under law, because we need no law. While the Spirit is leading us to love, we need no law to forbid us to hate. Law has power neither to command nor condemn those who are being led by the Spirit. Perhaps the best commentary on this verse is that of Paul himself in Romans 8:1-17.

V. 19 **Now the works of the flesh are plain** — If a man allows his own fleshly nature to have free rein in his life, he can look forward to the sins in the following list. These are not all the evils which the flesh can produce, but they are certainly enough to prove the point. Note that all these are characterized by selfish indulgence, rather than obedient surrender.

immorality — Immorality, or fornication, is a general word including all forms of unlawful sexual activity from adultery to homosexuality to prostitution. In New Testament times sexual standards among the Greeks and Romans were quite low. The Roman author Seneca noted that "Chastity is simply proof of ugliness," and that "innocence is not rare, it is non-existent." Gibbons has recorded that "of the first fifteen Emperors, Claudius was the only one whose taste in love was entirely correct." Among the Greeks, especially the philosophers, homosexuality was "the great national disease."

impurity — Impurity, or uncleanness, means general filth or defilement of one's moral being. It points to a dirty mind, dirty actions, and a dirty life. Hippocrates, the Father of Medicine, used this word to name the ugly accumulation around a festering sore or wound. The Greek Old Testament frequently used this same word in connection with the defilement that makes a man or woman unfit to come before the presence of God. In the New Testament it refers to a foul indecency of mind, or a spirit soiled and stained by the world.

licentiousness — This is the strongest and broadest term for moral indecency. Also translated lasciviousness or indecency, it names the reckless abandonment of what is decent and right. Josephus (*Antiquities*, XX, 5, 3) tells of a Roman soldier standing guard at a Temple ceremony in Jerusalem about 45 or 46 A.D. As if his very presence were not defiling enough, he publicly dropped his clothes and relieved himself, outraging public decency and recklessly defiling the sacred grounds. When a person is so corrupt that he neither cares about public respect, nor fears divine wrath, he has "licentiousness."

idolatry — Idolatry is literally "the worship of what can be seen." William Barclay says that to the ancients the idol had two functions: To localize and to visualize the god it represented. While some superstitious reverence was attached to the stone or wooden image, the people recognized that it was only a man-made representation of an unseen force. What they wanted was to tap the power of that force, or that god, for their own benefit. In order to gain good crops and fertile herds, they would worship the idol which represented the goddess of fertility.

Their worship, then, was actually a selfish greed to gain things for themselves. In this sense, Col. 3:5 says idolatry and covetousness are the same sin. The Lord God despises the sin of idolatry for two reasons:
1. It is a rejection to the true God. (Rom. 1:23)

CHAPTER 5 — GALATIANS 5:16-21

2. It is a worship prompted only by greed. (Col. 3:5) Idolatry is practiced today without visible idols.

V. 20 **sorcery** — Originally "sorcery" was the use of drugs, whether for good or evil purposes. Our modern pharmacy traces back to this word (Gk. *pharmakeia*) in its better sense. The word was always used in its evil sense in the Greek Old Testament, being closely associated with witchcraft (See Ex. 7:11 & 22; Isa. 47:9 & 12). Sorcery is an attempt to gain mastery over another person's life by occult means, especially the use of incantations and drugs.

enmity — Enmity is the exact opposite of *agape* love (See 5:22). In another form, this same word is the common Greek term for "enemy." It refers to an attitude of automatic hostility, such as Jews felt toward all non-Jews, and Greeks felt toward non-Greeks. While love ignores the faults and reaches out, enmity ignores the virtues and shrinks back. It is self-preservation at its fleshly worst.

strife — Strife is the outward result of inner hostility or enmity. It involves quarreling, squabbling, and general conflict. How unfortunate that this word could so accurately describe at least one early church (I Cor. 1:11; 3:3)!

In Greek mythology, Strife (Gk. *eris*) was the goddess of discord. Enraged because she was the only deity not invited to a certain marriage feast, she threw into the midst of the guests a golden apple inscribed "to the fairest." When no fewer than three goddesses claimed the apple, such discord and strife arose among the gods that it spilled over into human affairs and started the famous Trojan war. While only a myth, the story well illustrates the meaning of Strife.

jealousy — Jealousy was a word with both a good and a bad sense. In the good sense it was "zeal," a passionate desire or devotion to a noble end. However, since this fervor for a cause is easily perverted into selfish ambition, the word takes on a frequent bad sense. A competitive spirit may produce excellence, but it may also produce jealousy toward the success of someone else. Then the competitor no longer wants to achieve his own glories, but wants to take those achieved by another.

anger — Anger is another word that once had a noble side, but turned bad. (This is what always happens to flesh when it is totally uncontrolled by Spirit!) Although the word once meant courage and strong spirit, by New Testament times it came to mean a sudden outburst of bad temper or wrath. The fact that this wrath explodes quickly and then may be over in no way makes it a virtue.

The person who has vomited up all his rage on everyone around him will usually feel better for "getting it out of his system." This may help him (self-preservation of the flesh), but what about all those upon whom he has spewed his wrath? Is this the way of love?

Neither is the solution to try to bottle up the anger. The pent-up rage will eat like an acid inside a man, until he is finally destroyed. The only solution is to let Jesus drink that bitter cup for us. He alone can convert our bitter anger into better love.

selfishness — This word is also translated as "factions" (KJV) and "selfish ambition" (NEB). The word originally meant to work for pay. It soon came to mean the willingness to do practically anything, solely for what one could get out of it for himself. Aristotle used the word in reference to politicians who sought power and prestige, rather than a place to serve their people. The vengeful selfishness of the word is well seen in Phil. 1:17, where some were preaching Christ out of "partisanship," seeking only their own gain and hoping to cause trouble for Paul.

dissension — The Greek word for dissension or divisions means literally "to stand apart." This is the opposite of the Christian ideals of peace and fellowship. Division is directly contrary to God's plan and purpose for mankind. In fact, the final plan for the end of the ages calls for the reconciliation of all things in heaven and on earth (Col. 2:20; Eph. 1:10). When all things are put right with God, they will necessarily be put right with one another.

Today the church of Christ is racked with divisions, which cannot be justified. When God's children divide from one another, they are exercising the will of their former nature, which we know as the flesh.

party spirit — This comes from the verb meaning "I choose." When someone chooses a viewpoint different from what is accepted as true, he is called a "heretic" and his belief is "heresy." (Thus the KJV translation of this word.) In the New Testament, however, the primary meaning has to do with choosing up sides and forming a distinctive sect.

Forming an exclusive party around a pet doctrine is sinful even if that doctrine is true!

V. 21 **envy** — Envy is a genuine feeling of malice toward another person. It is more than just jealousy. The jealous man wants the gain that another man got; the envious man just wants to see the other man deprived.

The old "dog in the manger" fable well describes this kind of envy. The dog does not want and cannot use the hay in that manger, but it is determined to keep away the animals that could use it. When a man is unhappy so long as his neighbor is happy, he is guilty of this sin.

Jealousy says, "I want what you have."

Envy says, "I just don't want you to have."

drunkenness — This word is plural in the Greek, apparently referring to repeated instances of intoxication. Although wine was a universal drink throughout the Mediterranean world, drunkenness was widely recognized as wrong. Jews, Greeks, Romans — all diluted their natural

CHAPTER 5   GALATIANS 5:16-21

wine with water to avoid intoxication. If someone deliberately wanted to get drunk, he left out part or all of the water.

It is often asserted that alcoholism is a disease, and should be pitied, not preached against. Alcoholism may be a disease, but drunkenness is a sin! Perhaps some men have a lower tolerance for alcohol than others, but all men should know that intoxication is sin.

carousing — This word is also plural, and could be translated orgies. It refers to the shameful celebrations of the perversion of man's natural appetites for food, drink, and sexual fulfillment.

In II Maccabees is related the attempt of the Syrian ruler Antiochus Epiphanes to bring an end to Judaism. He made it punishable by death to observe the Sabbath or possess a copy of the Torah. He made a burnt offering of swine on the sacred altar. Then he made the Temple a house of prostitution. In II Macc. 6:4 it says that the Temple was filled with riot and "carousing."

I warn you, as I warned you before — The solemn repetition serves to underscore the seriousness of this matter.

those who do such things — The Greek tense of the word "do" indicates that Paul has in mind the continuing practice that develops into permanent habits. To whatever extent we may still find traces of these vices, we must labor with God's Spirit to eliminate them.

shall not inherit the kingdom of God — Sinful attitudes may escape the notice of men, but not God. If someone's real desire and direction for life is characterized by the works of the flesh, he will not go to heaven. Despite appearances to the contrary, he is not really a child of God, nor a member of the body of Christ. Consequently, if such be the case, he has no inheritance rights.

STUDY QUESTIONS:

1. Are physical appetites always evil?
2. How are the desires of the flesh in conflict with the desires of the Spirit?
3. Can you think of illustrations in the Old Testament for each of the works of the flesh?
4. How is idolatry like covetousness?
5. Why is a nice little sin like losing your temper grouped with such big bad sins as fornication and idolatry?
6. What is the true New Testament sense of the word "heresy"?
7. How is envy worse than jealousy?
8. What is the difference between an alcoholic and a drunk?
9. Which work of the flesh would you admit to be a trouble area for

THIRTEEN LESSONS ON GALATIANS

you? What are you going to do about it?
10. Since this group of sins is obviously not exhaustive, why do you suppose Paul chose these for this context?

Lesson Eleven

(5:22-26)

Fruit of the Spirit

22 But the fruit of the Spirit is love, joy, peace, patience, kindness, goodness, faithfulness, 23 gentleness, self-control; against such there is no law. 24 And those who belong to Christ Jesus have crucified the flesh with its passions and desires.

25 If we live by the Spirit, let us also walk by the Spirit. 26 Let us have no self-conceit, no provoking of one another, no envy of one another.

God did not intend that the works of the flesh should be weeded from our lives, only to leave us barren and empty. He has a wonderful crop to plant, where once weeds prevailed. The bountiful harvest of Christ-like virtues is what Paul calls the fruit of the Spirit.

V. 22 **But the fruit of the Spirit** — Standing in stark contrast to the selfish works of the flesh are nine virtues called the fruit of the Spirit. The word "fruit" is singular, indicating that all the virtues together form one composite harvest. We are not to sample two or three from a "spiritual smorgasbord," but rather to let the Spirit produce in us the full harvest.

love — Love is the first and greatest of all Christian virtues (I Cor. 13:13). It is the very nature of God (I John 4:8) and the essence of Christ's

THIRTEEN LESSONS ON GALATIANS

commandments (I John 3:23; 4:7-11, 19-21).

The Greeks had four separate words for love, which may be briefly described as follows:

Eros (EH roce) — Passionate sexual love
Storge (stor GAY) — Family love and devotion
Philia (fih LEE ah) — Friendship and affection
Agape (ah GAH pay) — Care and concern

The Greeks did not hold *agape* love in high esteem, so they rarely used the word. Its full beauty and meaning was not developed until its use in the New Testament as God's kind of love. There it is seen to be the highest and strongest love of all.

The Stoics were the leading philosophers of Jesus' day. They taught that it is dangerous to love. Epictetus said a man should teach himself not to care if he lost a pottery cup, or a dog, or even a piece of land. Eventually he could lose his health, his children, his wife — and not care. This would be the ultimate, unshakable happiness!

Aristotle taught that love is diluted when widely shared. He said one must draw a tight circle about himself and a chosen few to know real love.

Jesus totally reversed these concepts. He demonstrated that real love is willing to risk everything, and that real love cannot be restricted and self-centered. The greatest love draws the most inclusive circle.

An interesting contrast can be drawn between the three major concepts of love. Whether ancient or modern, these same forms of love can be found:

Eros says, "I love *only if* you make me happy."
Philia says, "I love you *because* you are so lovable."
Agape says, "I love you. Whether or not you make me happy . . . whether or not you are always lovable . . . I love you anyway."

As the Spirit re-creates us in the image of our Creator, we will have a love with these characteristics:

1. *Agape* loves even when love is not deserved (Rom. 5:8).
2. *Agape* loves without restrictions. It reaches out to meet the need wherever a need arises (I John 4:9-12).
3. *Agape* loves by choice and by will, not just by feeling and emotion. It is the only kind of love that can be commanded.
4. *Agape* loves without counting the cost, and without calculating its own profit.

joy — Joy is at the heart of the Gospel message. In the beginning the angels at Bethlehem heralded the "good news of great joy." At the end the risen Lord appeared to his disciples, who "disbelieved for joy" (Luke 24:41). The Gospel is such joyful good news that it really is hard to believe! (Note the contrasting absence of joy in legalism, such as

CHAPTER 5 — GALATIANS 5:22-26

was being taught in Galatia.)

Joy is a happiness that is spontaneous, radiant, and most of all, clean. The shrill, jaded laughter of the world cannot compare with the exuberant joy of the Spirit. Real joy is not prompted by happy circumstances, but triumphs over any circumstances. Always rejoice! (Cf. I Thess. 5:16; Phil. 4:4)

peace — The concept of peace comes into the New Testament with a rich background, both in Greek and Hebrew. The Greek word for peace refers to an absence of alienation, a state of reconciliation and oneness. The Greek philosophers were constantly seeking peace, but always in a negative way. For them peace meant removing pain, eliminating desire, and killing emotion. This produced a vacuum, not peace.

The Hebrew approach to peace was much more productive. *Shalom* is much more than the absence of conflict. It is the presence of all that is needed for man's highest good. For instance, when Joseph asked about the well-being of his father back in Palestine, he actually said, "Is it *shalom* with him?" (Gen. 43:27).

Peace is an inner sense of well-being. While joy is the mountaintop of happiness, peace is the plateau of contentment. Even if the Christian comes down at times from the highest peaks, he need not go into the valley of despair, for he can stay on the plateau of peace.

patience — The literal meaning of this word for patience is "long-tempered." It refers to the quality of temperament which does not quickly flare up and explode. The Apocalypse of Baruch says "wrath is restrained by longsuffering (patience), as if by a rein."

Two different words are often translated "patience" in the New Testament. Our word here means especially patience to put up with people, enduring their unforgivable stupidity. The other word, as in Romans 5:3, means endurance to outlast unpleasant circumstances.

Our perfect example of longsuffering is God Himself. In the days of Noah, God restrained His wrath while the ark was being prepared (I Pet. 3:20). In these present days, God is again restraining the wrath and punishment which the world deserves. The only reason He has not already destroyed this world is that He is "longsuffering (patient), not willing that any should perish" (II Pet. 3:9).

kindness — Kindness comes from a Greek word meaning "virtuous, excellent, and gracious." It is an inner beauty of spirit which blooms into sweet and loving Christian character. This kindness, however, is not only a sweet disposition — it is an active benevolence. It is not just the gentle voice stopping briefly by the bedside, it is the tender hand that stays to feed, to wash, to heal.

goodness — Goodness means moral uprightness. It is concerned with measuring up to the standards of right and wrong. The distinction between "kindness" and "goodness" can be found in Christian writers all the way back to Jerome in the 4th century. Goodness is Jesus cleansing the Temple and rebuking the Pharisees; kindness is Jesus reaching out to the woman at the well and to the little children.

Just think, though, how rarely these virtues are combined! One man is morally and doctrinally straight, but is harsh and cold in his faith. Another man is full of understanding and kindness, but finds no deviation from morality or truth ever serious enough to be condemned. We should find in Jesus our perfect example of the perfect blend — a generous goodness and a wholesome kindness.

faithfulness — Faithfulness was a common word in ancient times. It is found describing a slave who is "faithful and not given to running away." It is the usual word for the "pledges of loyalty" given by a defeated nation to a conquering king. Two good synonyms for faithfulness are loyalty and trustworthiness.

The KJV has here simply "faith," which to many people means merely the exercise of the mind in believing a certain fact. However, the word "faith" itself must include the element of loyalty. This can be seen even in English. To be "faithful" equals to be "full of faith." Just think, though, how many people claim to be "full of faith" and yet freely admit that they are not "faith-full"! What they are full of is not faith (loyal commitment based on trust and belief), but simply ideas about whether God probably exists or not.

V. 23 **gentleness** — Gentleness, or meekness, is one of the least understood words in the Bible. Meekness is not weakness, or lack of courage — in fact, it is just the opposite. Meekness is great strength or strong spirit held under control.

Two uses of gentleness in classical Greek illuminate its real meaning. Xenophon said that horses which had been wild, but were then trained to obey the reins, were "meek." Aristotle said that "meekness" was the golden mean between excessive anger and excessive apathy or spinelessness.

In the Bible only two men are called meek. In the Old Testament, it is Moses who is "very meek, more than all men who are upon the face of the earth" (Num. 12:3). Yet this same Moses had marched in before the most powerful man on earth and demanded, "Thus says the Lord, let my people go!" The man who led perhaps two million slaves to freedom was no weakling, no coward.

In the New Testament it is Jesus himself who is called meek (Matt. 11:29; 21:5). Yet Jesus was strong in every way. One need only see him cleansing the temple, confronting the Pharisees, or "setting his face toward Jerusalem" (Lk. 9:53), to know his strength.

In many ways meekness is like our "yield right-of-way" signs. Even

CHAPTER 5　　　　　　　　　　　　　　　　　　　　GALATIANS 5:22-26

when we have superior force and could bully our way through, we often yield our rights to our fellow man. He who is meek has yielded his reins to God and his rights to the well-being of others. He is gentle, teachable, and submissive to authority.

self-control — Self-control is the final part of the fruit of the Spirit. The word "temperance" used in the KJV gives many people the erroneous idea that this is merely to abstain from alcohol.

The root of this word means "to hold, to grip, to have power over." In this form it means mastery over the body's appetites, especially in the area of sex. The human body has appetites which are totally ignorant of right and wrong. One's stomach may crave food, regardless of whose food it is, what his diet may require, or whether the time is appropriate. The stomach is simply hungry; the reasoning mind must control. When a man is able to deny wrong desires and satisfy right desires, he has self-control.

The Christian ought not to expect desires to go away; he ought rather to gain mastery over them through the Spirit.

against such there is no law — Selfish flesh is always leading us into trouble and must be held back by law. The Spirit, on the other hand, urges us on to what is good, and does not need legal restraints. The more our own spirit is in tune with God's Spirit, the more freedom from law we have. Ultimate freedom allows us to do "anything we please," since what we please to do is the will of God.

V. 24　**those who belong to Christ Jesus** — This select group is made up of those who have:

　　　　1. Been rescued by Jesus (1:4).
　　　　2. Been justified by faith, not works of law (2:16).
　　　　3. Been crucified with Christ (2:20).
　　　　4. Been baptized into Christ and put on Christ (3:27).

have crucified the flesh — When we were crucified with Christ we died to the old life. The works of the flesh, along with the old law which restrained them, have been replaced by the fruit of the Spirit. Christ has set us free *from* our sinful nature, not *for* our sinful nature!

passions and desires — Both these words are morally neutral; they may be either good or bad. It is when they are totally under the domination of selfishness that they are evil.

V. 25　**If we live by the Spirit** — That is, if we have life from this source. The law certainly never made anyone alive, but the Spirit does.

let us also walk by the Spirit — Since the Spirit is the source of our life, He must also be guide and leader of our life. We walk by the Spirit when He controls our actions and our thoughts through His written message to us.

V. 26　**Let us have no self-conceit** — Self-conceit is the very epitome of the works of the flesh; it is the exact opposite of the fruit of the Spirit. The Christian does not live for himself — he lives for God, and for his fellow-man.

no provoking of one another — This is again characteristic of the works of the flesh. When people are full of self-conceit, they are irritating (provoking) and hard to get along with.

no envy of one another — This is the same word found in verse 21. The Christian should be generous in his attitude toward others, genuinely pleased with the good fortune and blessings that others may enjoy.

STUDY QUESTIONS:

1. Why is "fruit" of the Spirit singular?
2. How is *agape* love different from the usual kind of love known in this world?
3. Is it possible to have laughter without joy?
4. What did the Hebrews mean by peace (*shalom*)?
5. What is the difference between kindness and goodness? Which do you need more of?
6. Can faith be separated from faithfulness? Why?
7. What is the usual concept of meekness?
8. Why is self-control a better ideal than "If it feels good, do it"?
9. Find each element of the fruit of the Spirit in the life of Jesus.
10. What does verse 26 have to do with this lesson?

Lesson Twelve

(6:1-10)

Bear One Another's Burdens (6:1-5)

1 Brethren, if a man is overtaken in any trespass, you who are spiritual should restore him in a spirit of gentleness. Look to yourself, lest you too be tempted. 2 Bear one another's burdens, and so fulfill the law of Christ. 3 For if any one thinks he is something, when he is nothing, he deceives himself. 4 But let each one test his own work, and then his reason to boast will be in himself alone and not in his neighbor. 5 For each man will have to bear his own load.

The man who lives the liberated life does not live for his own flesh, but for his brothers and sisters (5:13). Paul now gives us some practical instructions on how to live for others. When we are led by the Spirit to live this kind of life, we fulfill the law of Christ — the only law we are under.

V. 1 **Brethren** — This final chapter begins and ends on this note. The first ten verses deal primarily with brotherly love. It is written on the assumption that at least some of the Galatian readers have accepted their correction concerning law and grace, and are ready for teaching about living the free Christian life.

if a man is overtaken — As in the situation that later developed in Corinth (I Cor. 5:1), sometimes a fellow Christian may be caught or detected in a serious trespass. Whenever this happens, other Christians should be concerned. They must not have the conceited and arrogant attitude mentioned in the verse just before this (5:26), but should be genuinely interested in restoring a brother.

in any trespass — A trespass is a misstep, or a falling along the way. It is not intended that a self-appointed vigilante group should hound other members about any and every shortcoming. Paul is talking about a serious offense that demands correction.

you who are spiritual — Notice that there are three requirements for those who are to help the fallen brother:
1. Must be spiritual
2. Must have spirit of gentleness
3. Must watch themselves, lest they be tempted.

A Christian congregation should be able to determine who has demonstrated spiritual maturity. The wisdom of the whole body should take precedence over the ambition of the self-appointed watchdog, as well as over the reluctance of a spiritually qualified man with false humility.

should restore him — The Greek word for "restore" is used for mending what is broken (Matt. 4:21), for teaching (Luke 6:40), and for equipping and training to bring to full maturity (Eph. 4:12). In most instances the elders of the congregation would be the logical ones to restore the broken or dislocated member of the Lord's body.

in a spirit of gentleness — This fruit of the Spirit is necessary in the one who is to correct a brother. It is very easy to become overbearing and offensive.

Look to yourself, lest you too be tempted — Just because a person is spiritual he is not immune to temptation. The power of Satan is all too real, and we can never safely let down our guard.

V. 2 Bear one another's burdens — In this immediate context the burdens we must help carry are the temptations to sin. If a brother is struggling with a certain temptation we should not act like he has leprosy and avoid him. We should be all the more eager to reach out to help him.

fulfil the law of Christ — And what is the law of Christ? His commandment is that we love one another (John 15:12). We have been freed from the law of Moses so that we can apply all our energies to this law. This single command fulfils all the earlier law (5:14), and goes far beyond that law.

V. 3 For if any one thinks he is something — This ties back to 5:26 again. The man who takes himself too seriously is operating from self-conceit and will act on the level of the works of the flesh. He will have nothing but contempt for the brother who is overtaken in a trespass. Being without sin, he will gladly cast the first stone.

when he is nothing — One of the greatest lessons we can ever learn

CHAPTER 6 GALATIANS 6:6-10

is that we are only sinners, and will never deserve the grace of God. God's greatest men learned this. (See David in Psalm 51, Paul in I Tim. 1:15, and John in I John 1:8-10.) It is only when we admit our spiritual bankruptcy that we shall see God (Matt. 5:3-12).

V. 4 **But let each one test his own work** — An honest appraisal of ourselves is always in order. For such virtues as may be found we should praise God and the Spirit which produced them. For such faults as may be found we sould ask forgiveness. Unless we are completely blind, such an appraisal should give us plenty to be humble about!

his reason to boast will be in himself alone and not in his neighbor — The reason to boast should be understood as a ground for satisfaction. There is a sense in which this feeling of satisfaction is wholesome and right, as when Paul felt good about preaching the Gospel and refusing the salary he deserved (I Cor. 9:1-18). Most of all, the lesson is this: If you are to have a feeling of satisfaction, let it be in your heaven-helped accomplishments, not in your neighbor's failure!

V. 5 **For each man will have to bear his own load** — At first glance there seems to be a contradiction between verse two and verse five, especially in the KJV. First we are told to "bear one another's burden," and then we are told that each man must "bear his own burden." The solution lies in the two different Greek words for burden. The burden of verse two is *baros,* which means "heavy, having great weight." The burden of verse five is *phortion,* which is the common word for one's usual freight or cargo.

Thus, we must all help one another in the oppressive burdens of life, but we also each have certain things for which we alone are responsible.

Sowing and Reaping (6:6-10)

6 Let him who is taught the word share all good things with him who teaches.

7 Do not be deceived; God is not mocked, for whatever a man sows, that he will also reap. 8 For he who sows to his own flesh will from the flesh reap corruption; but he who sows to the Spirit will from the Spirit reap eternal life. 9 And let us not grow weary in well-doing, for in due season we shall reap, if we do not lose heart. 10 So then, as we have opportunity, let us do good to all men, and especially to those who are of the household of faith.

V. 6 **Let him who is taught the word** — One way in which Christians can show brotherly love and "bear one another's burdens" is by paying those who preach and teach the Gospel. It is only right that the man who gives up other employment to spend full time preaching and teaching should have his physical needs met by the church (Matt. 10:9-10;

I Cor. 9:1-18; II Cor. 11:8-9; I Tim. 5:17-18). In fact, the Lord commanded that those who proclaim the gospel should get their living by the gospel (I Cor. 9:14).

share all good things — This includes many things other than money. Whatever material benefits are available should be freely shared with those who helped bring spiritual benefits (Cf. Rom. 15:27).

V. 7 **Do not be deceived; God is not mocked** — The Galatians must not think they can toy around with the preaching of the gospel. It is worth their money, but far more, it is worth their lives. A spiritual law of harvest is involved here and they must pay close attention. They must not think they can mock ("turn the nose up at") God and treat his gospel with contempt.

whatever a man sows, that he will also reap — This same principle is given in II Cor. 9:6 with specific application to giving money. Money is involved here in this text as well, but only as one application of a grander truth. It is not merely a matter of the pocketbook, but of the entire battle between the flesh and the Spirit. The Spirit must control every area of the Christian's life, including his finances. A man must not hold back any part of his life from the Spirit, thinking to pull the wool over God's eyes. The choice he makes concerning what and where to sow will decide his destiny.

V. 8 **For he who sows to his own flesh** — If the choice is to sow to his own flesh, then the man has chosen to serve Self. He has reversed the demand of Christ that all who follow Him must deny self (Matt. 16:24). Some people suppose that because they do not live in wealth and luxury that they are immune to the warning about sowing to the flesh. However, anytime a person cares more about what he wants than what God wants, he is guilty.

will from the flesh reap corruption — Just as the flesh itself will someday decay and putrefy, all who sow to the flesh will reap corruption. The god Self will lead them to an eternal kingdom where the worms of decay never die (Mark 9:48), and the fire of destruction cannot be quenched.

but he who sows to the Spirit — We sow to the Spirit by investing all our resources in Him. Our time, talent, treasure — and our very selves — are placed fully at His disposal. We must be willing to spend and be spent, trusting the judgment of God more than our own. Our primary concern must be to fill our life's storehouse with the fruit of the Spirit.

will from the Spirit reap eternal life — Anyone who tries to keep his life for himself will lose it, but anyone who gives up his life to the Lord will find it (Matt. 16:25). While the consequences of his choice may not become immediately obvious, they are certain and sure.

V. 9 **And let us not grow weary in well-doing** — In addition to the dangers of choosing money or choosing an immoral, fleshly life, there is one more danger: that we will just grow weary and do nothing. Especially if the going gets tough, we will be tempted to give up and quit. (The word for "grow weary" is also found describing the despair of a woman in the middle of a long, difficult childbirth.) Since we are doing what is right, we cannot quit.

for in due season we shall reap — One cannot gather the harvest before the time is ready. We must wait for God to reveal the appointed time of harvest, and trust His wisdom. The fact that the harvest is guaranteed should make us rejoice, and should give us renewed enthusiasm to "keep on keeping on."

if we do not lose heart — The picture is that of a muscle straining hard at a task. Finally, in defeat, the muscle lets go and becomes limp. This is what we must not do. The same warning is echoed in Hebrews 12:3, where the last word in the verse is the same as used here for "lose heart."

V. 10 **So then, as we have opportunity** — It is interesting that the same word in verse nine for the due season of reaping is now used for "opportunity." Perhaps Paul was using this play on words to remind us that we are usually looking for "the time" in the wrong way. Since we have no control over the time of reaping, we should be more concerned about the time of serving. The thought of brotherly love and "bearing one another's burdens" is still in mind.

let us do good to all men — Love is a demanding law. So long as there are still people in need — hungry, despairing, lost — love will never let us rest. The whole world becomes eligible to receive our "doing good." Every race and every nation is included in "all men."

especially to those who are of the household of faith — While we must stand ready to do good to all men, we have a special responsibility to help other Christians. They are fellow members of our family and their needs receive first notice. When famine struck the churches of Judea, gentile churches from as far away as Greece and Macedonia sent relief.

We have no precise guidelines for deciding the benevolence budget of the church. Exactly how we should balance the needs of fellow Christians against the needs of "all men" has not been prescribed. While the saints deserve special attention, the rest of mankind must not go forgotten.

STUDY QUESTIONS:

1. What kind of trespass needs the special treatment of verse one?
2. What are the three requirements for those who set out to restore a fallen brother?
3. What is the "law of Christ"?

THIRTEEN LESSONS ON GALATIANS

4. In what way should a man boast in himself and not in his neighbor?
5. What about bearing burdens: Are we to take care of our own or help each other?
6. Why should the student share "all good things" with his teacher?
7. How might a person mock God?
8. What is God's law of harvest?
9. What temptation does the Christian face in addition to the obvious temptations of money and immorality (vs. 9).
10. What is the role of the church in benevolence? What is your opinion (not binding on others!) regarding:
    a. United Fund or Community Chest?
    b. Salvation Army?
    c. International programs such as C.A.R.E.?
    d. Money for a Christian family whose house burned?
    e. Money for a local non-Christian family whose house burned?
    What principles or guidelines would you suggest in evaluating these appeals?

Lesson Thirteen

(6:11-18)

Above All — The Cross of Christ

11 See with what large letters I am writing to you with my own hand. 12 It is those who want to make a good showing in the flesh that would compel you to be circumcised, and only in order that they may not be persecuted for the cross of Christ. 13 For even those who receive circumcision do not themselves keep the law, but they desire to have you circumcised that they may glory in your flesh. 14 But far be it from me to glory except in the cross of our Lord Jesus Christ, by which the world has been crucified to me, and I to the world. 15 For neither circumcision counts for anything, nor uncircumcision, but a new creation. 16 Peace and mercy be upon all who walk by this rule, upon the Israel of God.

17 Henceforth let no man trouble me; for I bear on my body the marks of Jesus.

18 The grace of our Lord Jesus Christ be with your spirit, brethren. Amen.

Paul has reached the end of his epistle. He has proved his apostleship, offered his arguments, and explained his application. He now makes his closing remarks with a final warning and a shout of victory for the cross of Jesus Christ. With this he rests his case, and commends the Galatians to the grace of our Lord.

V. 11 See with what large letters I am writing to you with my own hand — It was Paul's practice to dictate to a secretary or amanuensis, who would then write each word down (See Romans 16:22). Now, at the close, Paul takes the pen into his own hand to write the final words. (He told the Thessalonians this was the mark of each of his letters — II Thess. 3:18.) Compared to the neat letters of the trained scribe, Paul wrote rather large, bold letters.

The translation of the KJV takes a different direction, "See how large a letter I have written." This is probably incorrect for two reasons:
1. The word "letters" in plural in the Greek.
2. Paul did not use the word "letter" for the messages he wrote, always preferring the word "epistle."

V. 12 those who want to make a good showing in the flesh — The word for "make a good showing" is found only here in the New Testament. It means literally "to have a lovely appearance" or "to look pretty to the eye." Paul launches a strong attack on his opponents, twice accusing their motives in this verse. For one, they promote circumcision to make a favorable appearance, and for another, they are doing it to escape persecution.

compel you to be circumcised — Their bad motives were producing bad actions — specifically the insistence upon circumcision. Furthermore, they were not merely suggesting or recommending the rite, they were compelling it! Notice how fiercely the legalists always enforce their own personal ideas!

only in order that they may not be persecuted — When certain Christians adopted the doctrine of circumcision, they blended in with traditional Judaism and escaped persecution. They were no longer regarded as a new and dangerous sect, but a harmless variation of Judaism, with whom the pagans were more comfortable.

We who have faced little physical persecution or torture should not underestimate the pressure the Galatian Christians felt.

for the cross of Christ — Without the cross of Christ Christianity would not be a cause of stumbling (I Cor. 1:23) and would be universally accepted as a pleasant collection of nice platitudes. With the cross, Christianity unyieldingly asserts several unpleasant truths:
1. Sin is real and demands punishment.
2. God sent His own Son to save people, and they must make some response.
3. No amount of doing good can atone for one's own sin.
4. No other religion is true.

V. 13 For even those who receive circumcision do not themselves keep the law — The supreme folly of the legalists was evident. While they insisted on keeping circumcision, the badge of the law, they ignored

CHAPTER 6   GALATIANS 6:11-18

much of the rest of the law. If a person is free to reject those parts of the law he does not like, obviously the whole law is of little importance.
   that they may glory in your flesh — The false teachers were motivated by the desire for glory (See 4:17). They saw in the cutting of the flesh a mark of victory. They cared little for God's law — they were collecting scalps! They who glory in the cut flesh of their converts are guilty of the work of the flesh — selfish ambition.
   V. 14 **But far be it from me to glory** — Unlike the false teachers, Paul had no desire to glory in what he could take from his converts. (The expression "God forbid" found in some versions is not authorized. The Greek words simply say, "By no means! May it never be!")
   except in the cross of our Lord Jesus Christ — What a strange thing in which to glory! The cross was an object of shame. It was an ugly means of executing the lowest criminals and slaves. (Try to imagine a hangman's noose in place of the cross. How would that look on your necklace? What would that do to the architecture of your church? Yet, this is how Christianity broke into the world of the 1st century.)
   The cross is the symbol of man's depravity and God's sufficiency. It is the perfect illustration of the failure of human works and the remedy of God s righteousness, which is available through faith in Christ. The cross is the tower of triumph for grace, and the seal of defeat for works.
   by which the world has been crucified to me — The cross makes the point at which the Christian is cut off from the world. Because of the cross the enticements of the world lose their appeal. Because of the cross the child of God no longer is subject to the rudimentary elements of this world.
   It is interesting that the scriptures also point to baptism as the separation of the believer from the old life (Romans 6:1-4). Actually, baptism and the cross are closely connected, since it is by baptism that we join Jesus in his death. It is the cross which makes baptism significant.
   V. 15 **For neither circumcision counts for anything** — Surely by now it is clear that the keeping of a law, such as circumcision, does not win God's favor.
   nor uncircumcision — Neither is uncircumcision the secret to earning God's favor. God favor is not to be earned at all. And God simply does not care whether a person is circumcised or not! (See also 5:6).
   but a new creation — God does not want to remodel the old man of flesh; He wants to make a new one! "If any one is in Christ, he is a new creation; the old has passed away, behold, the new has come." (II Cor. 5:17). The only thing that counts on the scoreboard of heaven is whether a man is in Christ Jesus, and is clothed in His righteousness.
   V. 16 **Peace and mercy be upon all who walk by this rule** — The rule or standard by which the Christian must walk is the truth contained

in the preceding verse, which summarizes the doctrine of the entire epistle. Upon the people who walk by (literally, "get in line with") this great truth, Paul pronounces two blessings: peace and mercy.

Since we are justified by faith, not works, we have peace with God (Rom. 5:1). We do not live in the constant fear of coming up one good work short on the Day of Judgment. We have peace with God and peace of mind. We have all that is needed for our well-being (See 5:22).

Being justified by faith, not works, is itself the expression of God's mercy. The loving Father saw that we could not save ourselves and took pity on us. He provided a way of salvation that depended not on our goodness, but His own.

upon the Israel of God — Those who are in Christ are God's chosen people. Although once people were born into this select group by physical ancestry, now people are born again into the chosen people by union with Christ. In other words, the Jews are no longer the Israel of God, the chosen people. "Not all who are descended from Israel belong to Israel, and not all are children of Abraham because they are his descendants" (Rom. 9:6-7).

God has not abandoned the Jews, however. They are still eligible to receive salvation, but on the same terms as the Gentiles. If a Jew (or a Gentile) wants to be numbered among God's chosen people, he must accept Jesus Christ as his Lord and be united with Him in His death. (Cf. Rom. 11:23) Those who are in Christ are the true Israel of God.

V. 17 **Henceforth** — In conclusion, and from now on.

let no man trouble me — Literally, "let no one give me hardships." What Paul has written should prove conclusively, once and for all, that his Gospel is true. There is no ground for his opponents to stand on. Their mouths have been stopped and their arguments have been silenced. Paul would like to hear nothing more from them.

for I bear on my body the marks of Jesus — The proof of Paul's character can be seen in what he has suffered.

"Five times I have received at the hands of the Jews the forty lashes less one. Three times I have been beaten with rods; once I was stoned. Three times I have been shipwrecked; a night and a day I have been adrift at sea; on frequent journeys, in danger from rivers, danger from robbers, danger from my own people, danger from Gentiles, danger in the city, danger in the wilderness, danger at sea, danger from false brethren, in toil and hardship, through many a sleepless night, in hunger and thirst, often without food, in cold and exposure." (II Cor. 11:24-27)

All this simply shows how extremely wrong it has been for Paul to be attacked by some of the Galatians.

V. 18 **The grace of our Lord Jesus Christ be with your spirit** — Paul's

CHAPTER 6   GALATIANS 6:11-18

concluding words, as always, are centered on the idea of grace. Grace is unmerited favor, which means that God is smiling down at us, even though we deserve his wrath. Grace is the granting of legal pardon through the atoning death of Jesus, even though we had no righteousness of our own. Grace is the end of the old law, and the death of the custodian (3:23-26). Grace is the coming of the Spirit into our lives, so that we are saved from the unfruitful works of the flesh and saved for the good fruit of the Spirit.

"By grace you have been saved through faith; and this is not your own doing, it is the gift of God — not because of works, lest any man should boast" (Eph. 2:8-9).

brethren — For the ninth and final time Paul addresses his readers as "brethren." Even though he has scolded and rebuked them, warning them of the consequences of apostasy, he still counts them his brothers. While some of the Galatians may have been lost to the Judaizers, Paul seems hopeful of the successful recovery of the majority.

Amen — "So be it."

STUDY QUESTIONS:

1. Why did Paul mention the "large letters" written with his own hand?
2. In what ways did Paul accuse the motives of the false teachers in Galatia?
3. How did the acceptance of the law of circumcision help certain people to avoid persecution?
4. What does it mean to "glory in the cross of Christ"?
5. How are Christians and the world crucified to each other?
6. If neither circumcision nor uncircumcision mattered, why didn't Paul just let them go ahead and be circumcised?
7. Who is the true Israel of God?
8. What do "peace and mercy" have to do with the subject of this epistle?
9. How would you explain the concept of grace to a child?
10. What have you gained from the study of Galatians?